Creative Coaching

Jerry Lynch, PhD

Human Kinetics

Library of Congress Cataloging-in-Publication Data

Lynch, Jerry, 1942-
    Creative coaching / Jerry Lynch.
        p. cm.
    Includes index.
    ISBN: 0-7360-3327-0
    1. Coaching (Athletics) I. Title.

GV711 .L96 2001
796'.07'7–dc21   CIP
                                                                                  00-053932
ISBN: 0-7360-3327-0

Developmental Editor: Julie Rhoda; **Assistant Editor:** Carla Zych; **Copyeditor:** Jacqueline Blakely; **Proofreader:** Sarah Wiseman; **Indexer:** Craig Brown; **Graphic Designer:** Nancy Rasmus; **Graphic Artist:** Kim Maxey; **Photo Manager:** Clark Brooks; **Cover Designer:** Keith Blomberg; **Photographer (cover):** © Sarah E.M. Becking; **Photographers (interior):** Full credits on p. xiv; **Printer:** United Graphics

Human Kinetics books are available at special discounts for bulk purchase. Special editions or book excerpts can also be created to specification. For details, contact the Special Sales Manager at Human Kinetics.

Printed in the United States of America   10 9 8 7 6 5 4 3 2 1

Human Kinetics   Web site: www.humankinetics.com

United States: Human Kinetics
P.O. Box 5076
Champaign, IL 61825-5076
800-747-4457
e-mail: humank@hkusa.com

Canada: Human Kinetics
475 Devonshire Road Unit 100
Windsor, ON N8Y 2L5
800-465-7301 (in Canada only)
e-mail: hkcan@mnsi.net

Australia: Human Kinetics
57A Price Avenue
Lower Mitcham, South Australia 5062
08 8277 1555
e-mail: liahka@senet.com.au

Europe: Human Kinetics
Units C2/C3 Wira Business Park
West Park Ring Road
Leeds LS16 6EB, United Kingdom
+44 (0) 113 278 1708
e-mail: hk@hkeurope.com

New Zealand: Human Kinetics
P.O. Box 105-231, Auckland Central
09-523-3462
e-mail: hkp@ihug.co.nz

*To Dean Smith,
the quintessential creative coach
with a teacher's heart*

contents

Developing Qualities for Successful Leadership

Leading With a Purpose

Unleashing Prepared Athletes

foreword

Over the years, I have been fortunate to have a number of friends who have supported my development of coaching principles. I count Jerry Lynch as one who has given me encouragement and information to make a difference in helping athletes reach their potential. There have been a number of times that I have used Jerry's examples to support my journeys into the uncharted waters of coaching.

Jerry has worked hands-on with some young college coaches to form a spiritual community. He has written a number of books using Eastern thought—particularly the Tao—to show examples of the mind-spirit integration in athletics and in life in general. Although *Creative Coaching* doesn't refer to Oriental thought, Jerry's followers will certainly see its influence. As coaches, we must use the whole being in creating a coaching atmosphere. In developing a team and supporting our athletes, Jerry Lynch is right there in the midst of the moment, encouraging us to keep reaching toward the light.

—Phil Jackson

Teaching, Guiding, Motivating, and Winning

As I sit down to write this book, I can't help but reflect on how fortunate I am to have a career in athletics. As a sport psychologist and athletic development specialist, I get to work closely with coaches and athletes who strive to be their best in a passionate, competitive, fun environment. For me, it's a dream job, the continuation of my early years growing up as a gym rat in the heart of New York City. It's fun, exciting, and challenging.

Coaches who present a wide spectrum of coaching styles have taught me how to creatively motivate and inspire athletes and entire programs. I've taken all of this wisdom to heart, reflected on it, coupled it with my expertise in athletic development and sports psychology, and fashioned some exciting, creative ways to cultivate effective, winning leadership strategies for sport.

After 25 years of working with coaches and programs to motivate athletes, I now believe that consistently successful coaching is usually the by-product of a team's or athlete's success in the preparation phase—all those hours of practice and training. An equally important factor is a coach's ability to instill and inspire, in a nurturing environment, winning traits in athletes: enthusiasm, courage, compassion, tenacity, desire, belief, selflessness, and patience. These qualities ultimately become the glue that binds a team, the spark that ignites the spirit and passion within the athletes, enabling them to sustain high levels of performance during their competitive years and beyond. Creative coaching is about cultivating these qualities in yourself and finding ways to teach them to those you lead.

Times have changed in coaching over the past 25 years. Players seem to be more complex, less pliable, and more apt to fight for what they feel they deserve than they were in the Vince Lombardi or Woody Hayes era. Today, for example, athletes expect to be listened to and to be treated with respect; anything less is not tolerated by them or by administrators. Players have rights, as they always have, but today they are more inclined to embrace them and get what they deserve.

Athletes now are attracted to coaches who can treat them with respect, care, concern, and compassion, as individuals who have worth outside the playing arena. Over the years, I have polled more than two thousand athletes at the professional, Olympic, collegiate, and high school levels asking them why they need a coach. Most of them focused on the need for a coach to inspire, guide, encourage, and teach, to help athletes to be their very best. When asked how this is effectively accomplished, most agreed (to my surprise) that a coach needs to create an environment in which listening is possible, one that is based on respect and understanding. Such responses led me to conclude that coaches could benefit from some creative new methods of coaching to help fill this role.

When coaches look back, the moments that stand out—the times of extraordinary achievement and performance—are moments that occurred in an accepting, respectful environment. Creative coaches find innovative ways to develop positive, productive situations with more open communication with athletes and staff. This improved communication, in turn, enhances athletes' performance. For example, one Division I basketball coach listens to the same music as his athletes. He insists that doing so helps him to relate to his players on a more meaningful level and to understand each athlete as an individual with unique values and needs. Several coaches I've worked with have hired assistants who are closer in age to the athletes, which helps the coaching staff as a whole relate better to the players.

You may have noticed that many successful, well-respected coaches emphasize personal improvement, preparation, and the quality of play in addition to favorable outcomes. Legendary UCLA basketball coach John Wooden rarely talked to his players about winning or victory. Supposedly, he never referred to "beating" an opponent, although winning was important for him. Instead, he focused on preparation for extraordinary performance and urged athletes to do their best.

Successful coaches help athletes create situations in which risk-taking is a prerequisite of high-level performance. Creative coaches emphasize the importance of winning within the context of exploring and discovering one's full range of athletic and personal possibilities. Such creative coaching styles give athletes the opportunity to experience personal growth and competitive success.

Creative coaches are passionate, selfless, and focused on the good of those they lead. Different coaching styles can accommodate these character traits—you do not need to change the style that works for you. Instead, simply look for ways to instill these key concepts and creative methods into your existing repertoire. For example, consider John Hammond, assistant coach for the Los Angeles Clippers, and Mickey Wender, head swim coach at the University of Washington. Both coaches are very passionate, but they use two very different styles to communicate their passion. John is rather subdued, while Mickey is extremely outgoing and fiery in his approach. The athletes who play for both men, however, feel their coach's passion for their sport.

Creative coaches understand that the true battle in athletics has less to do with external events than with internal battles against losing enthusiasm, courage, fearlessness, and compassion. They are teachers who discover creative ways to instill these qualities and help their athletes cope with failures, mistakes, and setbacks. They create a program that seeks a winning tradition, knowing that loss is an essential ingredient on the road to success. And they truly love to win.

Athletics is an important part of everything you do as a coach. But the creative coach attempts to go beyond victory on the scoreboard to winning in the bigger game of life, helping athletes to discover their full potential. John Wooden once said that his responsibility as a coach was to help his players reach their full potential as human beings, and basketball was just a game to help them do this. Legendary football coach Alonzo Stagg said that whether or not he was successful wouldn't be known for another 20 years; that is, he was invested in victory both on and off the field as the athletes matured into adulthood.

Creative Coaching is a strategic handbook that addresses the challenges of coaching athletes for extraordinary performance. These precepts of leadership emphasize ways in which you can help your athletes change their limiting attitudes and, as a result, dig deeper within themselves and perform their best. The tactics I'll discuss can help you teach athletes how to live and play like champions.

At the end of each chapter you will notice a series of bulleted expressions. These are affirmations, words that reinforce the lessons to be learned and applied. They are action phrases that, repeated often, will help to create behavioral change. You may want to record these expressions on index cards and read them daily until they become part of who you are and what you do as a coach. Place the cards in your locker or on your desk at work to help you remain vigilant about putting these important precepts to use.

Throughout each chapter I have set apart key points from the text, quotes that emphasize content and serve as touchstones that will help you to remember what's most important. When you return to a previously read chapter, these quotes will provide for you a quick summary of what was covered. As with the affirmations, you may find it helpful to record these words on index cards and refer to them often.

My hope is that this book will complement and supplement your present level of skills and help you to be a more creative coach. May it ignite the flame of enthusiasm and excitement for your work while enabling you to nurture confidence, self-esteem, and courage in your athletes.

Alway remember how fortunate we are to be in this profession. The insightful words of the late college basketball coach Jim Valvano speak for all of us: "Other people go to an office. I get to coach. I know I've been blessed."

It's exciting to think about taking your professional life up a notch or two, especially if you have been thinking (as I do on occasion) that you're stuck in one place. *Creative Coaching* will nudge you in this direction in your work with athletes. Have fun, and let me know what you think by contacting me at the TaoSports Center via e-mail at **taosports@aol.com** or by calling 831-466-3031. Your comments are the seeds for my own professional growth. I couldn't do this work without you.

acknowledgments

Thank you to the coaches and athletes with whom I have worked over the years for teaching me all that I need to know in order to be helpful to you; you know who you are.

Thank you to Julie Rhoda and Ted Miller at Human Kinetics for teaching me how to rewrite a book and for helping me to create something much greater than what I had originally envisioned.

Thank you to Jan for teaching me to see the bigger picture, a perspective that enabled me to persevere and to see this project to its completion.

photo credits

part I

Developing Qualities for Successful Leadership

1

Cultivating Character

Never compromise what you believe to be right.

What you achieve in athletics is directly related to the depth of your coaching character—the way you coach, and whether you lead from your heart. This is not simply a matter of your chosen coaching style; to be successful, you must superimpose your unique personality traits on strong underlying qualities of character that reflect uncompromising principles. Florida State University's Bobby Bowden is a good example of a coach in whom "what you see is what you get." Bowden disarms even his opponents with his sense of humor and simple values. When he stood before five thousand of his peers at a coaching convention and claimed that his greatest strategic advice for defending long passes was to "back up," serious note-takers cracked up with laughter.

A six-month bout of rheumatic fever and the harsh realities of World War II put things into proper perspective for Bowden in his early teen years. His remarkable achievements as a coach have not shaken that solid moral foundation. His commitment to family, firmly held faith, and love of people are as genuine as FSU's status among the elite college football programs in the nation.

Players respond to Bowden immediately, recognizing his genuineness. Recruits and their parents compare Bowden to his less assured or less forthright peers and thereafter commit to the Tallahassee school. Have all of his athletes always demonstrated the values Bowden lives by and espouses? No. But that could be said of any coach in the modern sport era. What is so refreshing about Bowden is that despite all the publicity, scrutiny, and money that have come with national championships, he has remained the open, honest, and unaffected person he was when he started coaching at Samford in 1959.

Character is a virtue, something that is indicative of moral strength, goodness, personal integrity, and conscience. It is the essence of this chapter and the keystone of creative coaching. In this chapter you will learn how humility, flexibility, acceptance, fairness, and integrity are important components of character, and you'll learn how coaches who strengthen these traits and creatively instill them in their athletes become successful.

Your words and actions are the manifestation of your character—so if you want your athletes to trust you, be a trustworthy person. Don't promise more than you can deliver, and don't say things you don't mean. Such mixed messages confuse athletes. College coaches sign recruits by promising they'll be impact players in the program and will get plenty of minutes. However, once an athlete is committed, if it turns out that he is more valuable to the staff and team in a role that is different than what was promised, the staff will use the athlete as they see fit, regardless of the promise. Better for a coach to say how much he would like to coach an athlete and state a vision for the player, assuming everything works out as expected. It's tempting to promise the moon, but no one can predict the future. Promise instead that you and the staff will work diligently to create opportunities for the athlete to grow and improve.

When athletes see cracks in the dam of a coach's character, and therefore the program's integrity, they may choose various routes to safety. Some will remain with the program but "check out" emotionally, making it unlikely that they'll live up to their athletic potential while in that environment. Others choose to leave the program for the promise of something better elsewhere.

On the other hand, coaches who demonstrate impeccable character wind up with athletes who, barring outside pressures, stay with their team and play with heart. Not only is this commitment to a program better for the team in the long run, it also benefits the individual athlete's development as well; athletes tend to play better in environments that are predictably safe and secure.

Athletes are usually more relaxed, focused, and willing to "go the distance" with coaches of good character. We all perform at higher levels when we're in a safe environment. For example, Dean Smith, former head basketball coach at North Carolina, is widely acknowledged as having set the standard for coaches who lead with good moral character. He always treated his athletes with respect—as grown, responsible men who deserved to be trusted, listened to, and cared for. He was always fair yet firm in carrying out the rules of his program. The star of the team received the same treatment as those who rode the bench. Because he treated them well, Smith's athletes were able to play up to their potential.

You might be thinking to yourself that good character alone certainly cannot ensure victory on the scoreboard. You're right. Some of the best, most respectful, fairest people on earth could not produce a championship team to save their souls. Moreover, many unethical coaches have won major championships. But if you look at the pool of coaches who have been most successful, you will find that competent coaches with good character will get more from athletes than coaches with questionable ethics. Character may not help a coach to create the best athletic team, but it will help that team to be the best it can be.

When you lead your coaching with good character, you'll feel confident in your ability to develop champions, to lead effectively, and to experience consistent success. Staying in touch with the power that comes from character diminishes your fear, tension, and anxiety; it will drive you to seek and achieve continual excellence in all that you do.

Discover Your Character Strengths

It's helpful to determine which of the character traits you demonstrate in your coaching are your strongest and which are your weakest. One creative way to go about this is to open up the questions to your athletes and peers. Have them answer the following questions anonymously:

What are my best traits as a coach?

What aspects of my coaching do I need to improve?

Look for patterns in the responses. Is there one trait that several respondents cited as your strongest point? Is there one trait that stands out—a unanimously agreed-on trait? If over half of the athletes respond with the same complaint or criticism, you should definitely be concerned. You can decide to take concrete steps to change this trait, as it's likely a hindrance to effective coaching. By conducting such a survey, you communicate your openness to improvement and change, a strong character trait in itself.

There is no particular combination of character traits that makes a coach great. You must do what is comfortable for you, and even experiment from time to time to determine what is and is not comfortable. New coaches find that they experiment quite a bit with different styles; in time they learn what is a good fit for them. Consistency then follows.

Several coaches I have worked with attribute their coaching success to being true to their basic nature—whether that means being shy, opinionated, strong-willed, talkative, direct, or humorous—and expressing this nature through character traits they know to be right: honesty, fairness, kindness, respect, and patience.

Athletes will be loyal and reliable
if you model what you expect from them.
Discuss the specific aspects of character you expect
and how such traits might be demonstrated.

Dale Brown, nationally respected basketball coach at Louisiana State University, has said that to be successful as a coach, you need to be yourself—whether this means stern or cordial. In Bill Libby's *The Coaches,* Brown notes that "there is no clear way to succeed. One cannot copy another who's a winner. . . . Those who have succeeded and those who have failed represent all kinds—young and old, inexperienced and experienced, hard and soft, tough and gentle, good-natured and foul-tempered, proud and profane, articulate and inarticulate, even dedicated and casual" (preface, page v).

John Wooden and Adolph Rupp were two of the winningest coaches in college basketball history. Yet each had very distinctive personalities that translated to stark differences in their approaches to coaching.

Rupp, the "Baron of the Bluegrass" at the University of Kentucky for 41 years, had an aggressive, sometimes abrasive demeanor. His teams were equally hard-driving; they were relentless, running warriors on the court. And Rupp would stand for no less, as when his UK squad led 34-4 at halftime of a game and the coach demanded that his troops clamp down on the lone scorer on the opposing team, who Rupp said was "running absolutely wild." Little surprise that one of Rupp's players was NBA coach Pat Riley, who brings a similarly strong personality and tough-playing approach to the game.

Contrast that with the Wizard of Westwood, John Wooden, the former Purdue All-American who taught English and coached at the high school level for 11 years after graduating college. Wooden brought his modest Midwest demeanor and highly-tuned attention to detail to the UCLA campus in the late 1940s, and 27 years later left after having won a record 10 national championships and having made a profound impact on the game. The picture of Wooden, with perfectly erect posture intently watching from his seat on the sideline, game program rolled up in one hand, calmly providing directions to an assistant or instructions to a player is a far cry from the active, highly-charged picture presented by many coaches. Wooden believed that the players, not the coaches, should be the center of attention, and that if proper guidance was given at practice, the coaches should have little to say during games, anyway. So, game after game, his UCLA teams executed set plays with precision, just as the maestro had directed in the quiet of the practice gym. A quiet but self-demanding and intelligent role player like Keith (Jamal) Wilkes thrived in Wooden's disciplined system.

Only by knowing what our core values are can we act appropriately. Take some time to go for a walk or just sit quietly and reflect on the following list of traits. Ask yourself not only whether you value these traits, but whether you act on them. If you don't, can you find opportunities to strengthen them?

These are some of the main tenets of character; perhaps you can add others. Jot down next to each trait (and any others you have added) an example of how you demonstrate it in your daily coaching. If you don't demonstrate this in your coaching now, how could you do so in your coaching and other aspects of your life? Make your own list and place it where you will see it every day.

Truthfulness   _____

                 _____

Honesty   _____

                 _____

Kindness   _____

                 _____

Patience   _____

                 _____

Dependability   _____

                 _____

Consistency   _____

                 _____

Openness   _____

                 _____

Humility   _____

                 _____

Fairness   _____

                 _____

Try coach Chris Weller's hands-on approach to character development.

Chris Weller, head coach of women's basketball at the University of Maryland, believes in this approach. She writes words like *courageous, fearless,* and *compassionate* on cards and places them in her office—and her program exhibits these same characteristics. Coach Weller also creates a poster with words chosen by each of her athletes, each athlete's name appearing by the word she chose. Before going out to play, the athletes touch "their" word and recite it silently to themselves. These words are also used as concepts for team discussion on a weekly basis.

Perhaps these traits are qualities you would like *your* athletes to focus on, or perhaps you have others in mind. Print them out on large cards and hang them in the locker room and other visible places. Use them as Coach Weller has, or in your own ways, to help shape your program.

Let's look at some specific practices that will help you do a better job of focusing on and improving character.

Zone In on Your Purpose

The first step in improving your coaching character is to define a purpose that is greater than the needs or wants of any one person. Ask yourself this: *What is the team's mission?* For example, it's one thing to have a goal of winning a national championship or a conference crown but quite another to have as your mission raising the bar on the team's level of play.

You must truly *want* to achieve the goal; it must be fulfilling and have an element of passion. It must inspire you with the enthusiasm and determination to do whatever is necessary to achieve it. It should encompass the specific things that you commit to doing each day to achieve, answering the question *What do I need to do and how do I need to be to prove that I am serious about getting better?* A goal (or series of goals) will keep you on track in achieving your mission. Theoretically, if you accomplish each goal, your mission will be realized.

Your mission includes all those things team members are willing to do to demonstrate how serious they are about improving. For example, I will ask an athlete, "What four or five things are you willing to commit to doing in practice or in competition that will help you to compete at a higher level?" Sprint back on defense every time? Always dive for the loose ball? Surge to stay with an opponent who attempts to pass you for the win? These concrete behaviors force athletes to focus on the *process* of their playing and, as a result, on fulfilling the mission of being the best they can be.

The University of Maryland women's lacrosse team continually raises the standard by which they measure their success. They haven't focused solely on winning a national championship (though they achieved their sixth consecutive one in 2000) or on beating their rivals Virginia, North Carolina, or Princeton; instead, their mission has been to continue finding *ways* to raise the bar from the previous half, game, or season. More specifically, they concentrate on what they need to do or on how they need to be to demonstrate improvement over the recent past, and on how to go out and execute the plan.

They wanted to win the national championship, but they focused on the "little things" necessary to get that job done. For example, each athlete was very clear about what she had to do to improve defensively and offensively. As long as she did this (her mission), her level of play improved consistently. This new focus excited the players and the coaches, and as a result practices and games were flooded with enthusiasm. The coaching staff focused on maintaining this flow of enthusiasm by finding ways to help each athlete better her personal practice sessions and games each week of the season. Athletes were excited with their success in meeting doable stepping-stone goals as they improved their games one piece at a time.

To keep this enthusiasm strong throughout the season, I suggested to head coach Cindy Timchal that the individual athletes commit to three personal goals for each week of practice that would prove that they were serious about raising that bar. The goals were simply guidelines to keep them on track, touchstones to help them focus on the present moment—for example, showing up early for practice and staying late, going hard during drills, and encouraging teammates.

To increase team accountability, the staff created a list of these goals with each athlete's name and passed them around to the team. The coaching staff personally held the athletes accountable for choosing specific aspects of their game to focus on. Their behaviors and actions were recorded on sheets of paper and distributed to all members of the team, so everyone knew what was taking place. The controlled focus helped the team to sustain their enthusiasm.

The clarity of this team's mission and the reinforcing steps they followed every day at practice throughout the season enabled them to succeed. That season culminated in their sixth consecutive national title. The team won the championship, setting numerous records for scoring and defense in the process. Moreover, their enthusiasm continued, carrying over to their off-season training and into the following year. They came back supercharged and ready to begin raising the bar even higher.

This success can happen when you are clear about your team's mission. If you are unclear as to your mission or unable to communicate it effectively, athletes will focus on winning as their sole mission—an outcome that can't be controlled and therefore leads to anxiety and tension.

Focus on the Positive

Once you zone in on your team's purpose, your demeanor toward the mission can carry your message on. An enthusiastic coach can greatly enhance the energy level of an athlete and a team in this way. Just as you reinforce the purpose and fulfillment of the mission each day in practice by focusing on those aspects of the game that will help them achieve the mission, you cultivate enthusiasm by dwelling on what's good *each day*. For example, each day at practice it's important to catch your athletes doing what's *right* and to praise them for it.

Certainly, practices are environments in which coaches correct athletes' mistakes and tell them how they can improve so that they avoid crucial mistakes in game situations. But to focus *only* on what they are doing wrong creates a pessimistic environment that will douse the fires of enthusiasm. A head coach at Stanford University once told his staff and athletes that when things are going well, they should be on the lookout for problems, as this is when bad things usually happen. Such negativity breeds bad feelings, uses precious emotional energy, and creates passive-aggressive behaviors in athletes. His team was deprived of day-to-day positive reinforcement for their good work, and their performance suffered as a result of their tenseness. Other teams wondered why this odds-on favorite to win a national championship failed in their pursuit, given their extraordinary talent. The answer is simple. In that environment of fear, looking for anything to go wrong became a self-fulfilling prophecy; coaches and athletes became cautious, tight, and tentative, sabotaging their prospects for a national championship.

This is not to say that coaches can't critique athletes, help them improve, and handle behavior problems effectively. You can do all those things creatively and constructively by starting out with positive feedback about performance or behavior—*then* following that with suggestions for improvement. The positive observation opens the athlete to the possibility of making changes. Rather than saying, "Don't do this," try using the phrase, "You'll be even better if you do this." Chapter 2 provides additional methods of incorporating this positive focus in your day-to-day communication with your athletes and the other coaches on your staff.

Maintain Humility

Phil Jackson, former coach of the six-time world champion Chicago Bulls and current coach of the Los Angeles Lakers, has stated about his tremendous team success with the Bulls, "My record is more a team accomplishment than an individual one." He's not simply being humble for humility's sake. He honestly, genuinely sees the total team effort; this is part of his character. Jackson refused to be flamboyant as he quietly carved his impressive position in the arena of NBA coaching. Few coaches would hesitate to admit that a coach is only as good as his team and that coaches couldn't do their magic without the athletes they work with. The humble, modest leader understands the interdependence between coach and athlete. It is a relationship of mutual fulfillment, in which both coach and athlete share a common goal and work together to attain it. Understanding this creates the real magic of interpersonal well-being. Both coach and athlete need to be able to recognize their mutual contributions on the road to greatness.

Humility and modesty are invaluable qualities to have while leading athletes. More than likely you have experienced pretense (your own or that of another coach) at some point in your career, only to learn how it can backfire. If you've also experienced the results of more humble leadership, in which a coach does good work, steps aside, and lets athletes experience the positive results, you understand the rewards of this approach.

Cindy Timchal has experienced the results of her humble leadership in working with athletes and staff to establish a women's lacrosse dynasty at Maryland. Though she has amassed a 169-12 record, with seven national championships in 10 years, Cindy gives credit to her athletes, who commit to doing whatever it takes to be their best, who sacrifice and suffer to get the job done. They display a level of loyalty and respect possible only in an environment of sincere humility. Coach Timchal's method of leading with humility is summed up in a poster on her office wall that states this: "... you will step aside and they will say 'we did it ourselves.'"

Joe Paterno, Penn State football coach, believes that one of the many ways to keep humility in a program is to not put names on the back of jerseys. Though Joe is one of the winningest coaches of all time and a football legend, he does not seek out the limelight and does not want attention directed solely at the individuals on his team. The entire program—its mission, standards, and goals— is more important than any one player. Humility is not only part of Joe's character but something that he instills in his players through his coaching.

Another example of humble leadership is exhibited by the former coach of the Indiana Pacers, Larry Bird. He realized that he didn't have the experience that most head coaches do, so he delegated authority to his assistant coaches, whom he recognized as experts in their areas. In fact, during most timeouts, the assistants talked to the players more than Coach Bird did. However, he still had the players' respect. He realized that this method was best for the team, and he didn't try to call all the shots or let his ego get in the way.

*Humble attitudes create loyalty
and are the foundation of success.*

Many coaches seem to have a dire need to promote themselves, an insecurity in their own worth that can be exceedingly harmful to the well-being of athletes, teams, other coaches, and athletic programs. If you're caught up in the process of self-promotion, it can become easy to overlook the needs of those you coach. You run the risk of being less effective in the work you have been hired to do: looking out for the welfare of those under your charge. The following exercise can help you practice humility and empower those you lead at the same time.

Call a team meeting and ask athletes to bring paper and pen. It's important to remind them that their responses will remain anonymous so they may provide a more open, honest reply. Ask them to respond to these two questions:

1. When talking with a recruit or any athlete wanting to play for this team, what would you tell them about

   a. the program,

   b. the coach(es), and

   c. the staff members?

2. If you could make any changes to the program, what would they be?

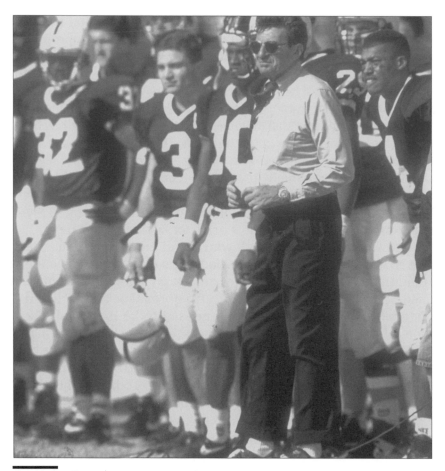

Coach Joe Paterno keeps the focus on the program rather than the players or the coach.

Collect the responses and have a disinterested person type them up. Then read all the responses and have your staff do the same. If a pattern is evident in the responses to any of the questions, consider changes you could make that would positively address the athletes' concerns. Discuss your ideas with the staff. Then discuss with the team the changes you and your staff would consider making and ask for their help in the process. You can further the dialogue between coaches and athletes by providing athletes with a list of changes that the coaching staff would like to see the team address to improve the program.

By conducting this survey, you send the message that the athletes' voices count and that you're willing to consider appropriate changes. You also make it clear that the staff is part of the team and deserves to be heard as well. In this situation, no one is too big to change. Humility is a two-way street. With an open mind and heart, you will often feel humble, knowing that you're not perfect and that the team (athletes and staff included) can be improved. The real benefit of this exercise is the potential impact for future success as the team, the coaches, and the staff become closer and more aligned with the direction in which they feel the team should move. It's humbling to hear the truth when it runs contrary to your biased opinions, yet this truth is often the foundation for stronger, more loyal relationships and less disruptive behavior from those you lead.

I know of a collegiate coach who found out through this exercise that his athletes felt he needed to take more time to understand them. They suggested that he hire younger staff members, or someone closer in age to them, so they could be better "heard." They felt that the generation gap needed to be tightened. They thought that the addition of a young assistant coach would make it easier for everyone to communicate, that he could act as a mediator who would carry concerns more constructively from the team to the coach (and perhaps vice versa). To his credit, when the timing was right, the coach hired such a person and has since experienced better communication between athletes and staff.

On the other hand, too many coaches blindly and arrogantly lead without valuable input from their athletes. Their approach is to dictate and to dominate, which ultimately results in their losing the respect and confidence of their teams. This style makes it difficult for athletes to go all out for their coach. Although some coaches who are known for using such an approach have produced champions, you'll notice that the consistency of effort and outcomes is poor. For example, consider the meltdowns that Indiana University's basketball team experienced in postseason play (Big Ten and NCAA tournaments) over the last five years of Bobby Knight's tenure there. By the end of each season, his athletes seemed emotionally and mentally exhausted by the strain of playing for him and didn't seem to have the will to win as a result. In contrast former University of Illinois coach Lon Kruger amassed an 8-2 record against Knight, often with teams of inferior or equal talent. A particularly dramatic illustration of the contrast between the two coaching styles occurred in a game between the two teams in February 1998. During the game, referee Ted Valentine gave Knight three technicals and ejected him from the game. Knight went ballistic. While chaos raged around Knight and the IU players, Kruger and the UI players huddled around him were an oasis of calm; Illinois went on to win the game handily.

In contrast, University of Arizona softball coach, Mike Candrea, long ago recognized the value of involving athletes in the communication and decision-making processes. In addition to being a highly knowledgeable teacher and tactician in his sport, Candrea has carved out an amazing winning record through his coaching career because he respects his athletes and allows them the freedom to excel. Where other coaches might harness their players, sticking to a rigid approach that may or may not apply to specific situations, Candrea unleashes the talents of his team and challenges them to exceed what even they think is possible.

Being humble is more potent in achieving your goals and in being successful than always trying to prove yourself. Successful coaches practice humility. Be conscious of what you do not know and don't assume that you always have the only or the best answer; rather be open to adopting new ways of expanding your expertise. When success comes, realize the contributions of all involved. You couldn't achieve success without the work of your staff and team, and the support of parents and fans, and they couldn't do it without your guidance and expertise.

Of course, some coaches naturally attract attention and are celebrities in their own right. Yet this can still be a situation where humility shines through. For example, University of Utah men's head basketball coach Rick Majerus always draws a crowd, whether it be for his physical stature, his sense of humor, or his coaching brilliance. His teams play a selfless, often flawless brand of basketball and have enjoyed great success. Though more high-profile offers have been waved before him, he has remained at Utah for many years. Of course, Rick was influenced by his mentor, Marquette coach Al McGuire. McGuire was a media magnet who drew all the attention from the beginning of his days at Marquette right through his last game, in which his team won the 1977 NCAA basketball championship.

Although he does not seek it, Rick Majerus gets plenty of attention from fans and members of the media.

Offer Acceptance

Accepting others is not an easy task for anyone, including coaches. Coaches may fear that an athlete who feels accepted and approved will see no need to change or improve when needed. On the contrary, athletes, like most people, are more likely to change if they feel accepted for who they are. When an athlete performs well, it is easier to accept and overlook less desirable behaviors. Yet it's important that you not wait until an athlete achieves success before you show acceptance of who she is and how she plays.

Do not base acceptance on achievement.
Communicate clearly that it's the person who counts.

Part of accepting your athletes is understanding that all of them, regardless of skill level, will have off days now and then. Off-the-court matters will occasionally affect an athlete's performance, no matter how hard he tries to focus on a competition. Acceptance also includes acknowledging the unique contribution each athlete makes to a team, whether it is a skill, a consistent work ethic, social chemistry, or overall positive attitude.

The bottom line is that an athlete should be accepted as a valuable person—but at the same time, the athlete needs to recognize that participation at a high level of sport is not a right but a privilege. A prerequisite for earning that privilege—and the difference between a program's success and failure—is understanding and accepting the effort required to fulfill one's team role. The coach who can creatively assign roles and motivate athletes to a high commitment in fulfilling them will be very successful. When assigning roles to athletes, you need to be sure they understand why that role is crucial to success, as this will help them to accept and commit to that role. (For more on roles within teams, see chapter 4.)

There are many ways to express your acceptance of an athlete in an everyday context. A simple remark such as, "Megan, I loved your effort in practice today. . . . glad you're here" takes no time at all. Asking your athletes direct, positive questions such as, "Chris, how's school going?" or "Caroline, what have you planned for your vacation?" or "What are you studying this week?" or "What are your goals?" shows your interest, respect, caring, kindness, and openness to hearing about what's going on with them. Make an effort to get to know each person and learn what is special about that person. Then, from time to time, tell them why they are special.

One of my favorite coaches who continually demonstrates caring and acceptance is Quin Snyder, head basketball coach at the University of Missouri. When I first worked with Quin, he was an associate head coach at Duke. He treated each athlete in a special way, whether he was a shining star, a "falling" star, or no star at all. During practice and games, he related to his athletes like no one else I've seen. He always had a special name for each athlete, a personal touch that would demonstrate his affection and caring. Chris Burgess was "Burg," Chris Carrawell was "C-well," and Steve Wojciechowski was "Wojo." Quin would often blow his whistle after a play in practice and shout to a player "I love the way you do that, I love it." Another favorite comment of his was "We need you. You're important to us." These young men would get on their knees and clean the floor for Quin if he asked; they truly respected him and felt comfortable under his leadership. He communicated deep love, caring, and acceptance through a sincere interest in who they were as people. The athletes appreciated having such an environment and played their hearts out because of it. Quin never let a chance go by to remind them how glad he was that they were part of the team. He was extremely busy yet found time to connect with everyone.

As a head coach at Missouri, not much has changed in Quin's coaching style. He continues to accept his athletes for where they are in their development while instilling in them the desire to improve and expand. Acceptance does not equal condoning or encouraging stagnation, and you can tell an athlete "You are developing into a better player every day, and I know you can be even better if you wish." This statement communicates acceptance and encouragement for change. Ironically, it's an environment of acceptance that creates the possibility for change.

All athletes need to feel accepted by their coaches. It motivates them to greater heights.

Consider the following ways that you can demonstrate acceptance of others.

- Listen. Everyone feels accepted when listened to. The message becomes clear: "I count."
- Tell an athlete why you are happy he is part of the team. Don't limit yourself to reasons of athletic achievement only; find personal reasons to show your acceptance.
- Use first names when addressing your athletes. No word is sweeter to a player's ear.
- Take the time to have regular, short meetings with individual athletes. Rather than the usual "sports talk" rap session, keep it personal—school, family, social life. Show that you care about life away from the court.
- Separate the person from the behavior; accept the person even though you may not approve of the behavior. For ex-

ample, you might say, "You're a terrific person; however, I can't tolerate your missing practice."

Another kind of acceptance requires that you realistically assess your team's capabilities and base performance expectations on these assessments. You can't expect a team to perform at high levels if they don't have the basic abilities. For example, Alan Kirkup, women's soccer coach at the University of Arkansas, had many years of success at Southern Methodist University (SMU), yet recently accepted the challenge of taking a less talented program at Arkansas to levels no one thought possible. Alan did not confuse acceptance of the team's current abilities with giving up. He simply said, "I will make the best of what I have and continue to go forward."

He has realistically assessed the need to recruit certain key players who will help his team to be in contention for a national title someday. Until then, he accepts his losses as learning opportunities for the young athletes as they improve and continue to nurture the dream of going the distance. By focusing on the team in this way, Alan has seen his athletes grow and develop as the season progresses. By the last game of his first season there, Arkansas gave the University of Florida (a top-three team nationally) a competitive game, and the players began to see that they could compete with the best. In just his second year there, his team was picked to win their conference division.

Accepting who you are, where you are in your coaching development, and the results that come your way are all part of this process. Some coaches are better at the high school level than the college level. Others are better as assistant coaches rather than as head coaches. In any case, many coaches spend their time in a grass-is-always-greener mind-set, looking to move to a higher level of competition or to assume a larger role where they are. Some of the most admirable and meaningful coaching jobs have been done by assistant coaches at the high school and college levels. For example, Tony Harvey, associate head basketball coach at Missouri, is one of the best recruiters in the game. He has a particular gift for talking with prospective athletes about the program and fills this important role admirably.

There's no need to become inert or inactive when you practice acceptance. Notice what is, accept it, then develop a plan to act accordingly. Move forward, improving and developing with what you have. For example, you can accept defeat in a gracious manner and set an example to your team and staff; this will help them learn from the defeat what they can improve next time and what they should feel proud of.

Acceptance enables you to let go of what you can't control and to take charge of what you can.

Acceptance also can mean making do with what you have. Many inner city coaches work with poorer facilities and equipment and fewer competitive options than coaches in the suburbs or towns where there is a high level of support for extracurricular activities. Football coach Bob Shannon made his mark at East St. Louis High School in one of the lowest-income, highest-crime areas in the country. Shannon somehow managed not just to survive, but to thrive, with six Illinois state championships. Moreover, Shannon earned great respect and admiration from his peers by fielding teams whose discipline and sportsmanship were very different from the behaviors to which his players were exposed in their neighborhoods. Parents of athletes who survived Sergeant Shannon's own form of boot camp could see the positive impact he made. Many of those players were able to gain college scholarships, earn degrees, and achieve success far beyond what was thought possible for young people from such an impoverished background.

And yet Shannon, too, reached a breaking point over differences with administrators, as well as the ongoing realities of coaching at a school that offered so little in the way of facilities, equipment, and salary. Although he is no longer at East St. Louis High, his work there is a shining example of what a coach can do under very poor circumstances to win championships and make a difference in athletes' lives.

Stay Flexible

Coaching is a profession with constant changes. Athletes come and go, injuries occur, motivations shift, rules change, weather turns, and schedules vary. Because of this, it is wise for you to create patterns in your daily work that help you to adapt to sudden shifts during a game, an event, or a season. Being flexible and open to change does not mean that you throw the values that you believe in—the essential elements of your character—out the window. Rather, being flexible is the ability to remain strong in your convictions while yielding on lesser points. The key to being appropriately flexible rather than too lenient is knowing that your convictions are deeply rooted standards that, if compromised, would take away from your integrity as a coach in your own eyes and in the eyes of your colleagues and athletes.

Some coaches' flexibility isn't always apparent to fans. For instance, Dallas Cowboy's legendary coach Tom Landry is regarded as one of the most stoic, expressionless coaches ever to walk the sidelines. Conversely, Bill Parcells was one of the most volatile and expressive coaches the NFL has ever seen. Both won Super Bowls and were highly successful leaders of their teams. Neither *seemed* to be forgiving or flexible. Their agendas and approaches were based on their deep convictions and standards, and were essentially set. Yet they were smart enough to listen to their athletes, to sift through outside input to find what was useful to them and their teams.

Landry's staid persona was almost worthy of a TV sitcom character. As an example, consider quarterback great, Roger Staubach's story about his former coach. "One time at Texas Stadium, we were driving, and I went to the sideline during a timeout to get the play. I was standing with him, waiting and waiting, while he looked up through that hole in the roof. Finally, he looked back at me and told me the play. As I started back on the field, I said, 'Coach, I always wondered where you got those plays.' I know he heard me. The other coaches were laughing. But he never changed expression."

At the same time, Landry did adapt to the changes taking place, and demonstrated a degree of flexibility that earned his players' respect. As Hall of Fame running back Tony Dorsett recalled, "I saw him loosen up as the years went by. He adjusted to a new generation of athletes, guys who wanted to know why before they did something. He became more relaxed on the practice field, and the players felt more relaxed in his presence."

Bill Parcells' teams played the way he coached, the way he demanded they play. With Parcells, it was all about control, so it is little wonder that his 1990 New York Giants team set a Super Bowl record for time of possession in beating the Buffalo Bills. The classic Type A personality, Parcells never appeared pleased, satisfied, or content. His standards were high and the toll it took on himself, mentally and physically, and his players, was sometimes excessive. Yet he also engendered a very high sense of loyalty in those who strived to meet his demands. And rebels like all-time great linebacker Lawrence Taylor found Parcells forgiving of those who demonstrated to their coach a total effort to the cause.

Perhaps the part of coaching that calls for constant flexibility is devising a game plan based on scouting reports about your opponent. You begin the contest only to be surprised by a "new look" in their offense—for example, an unusual stall tactic. What do you do? Do you stick with the original plan you devised based on what you gleaned from the scouting reports? Or do you adapt and figure out quickly how to settle into a different approach for dealing with the stall tactic by incorporating fast breaks and sprints on offense? Being rigid in your attack can quickly lead to destruction. It's best to think fluidly and to be ready to shift with the tide as necessary.

Your strength and power as a coach will increase with your ability to be flexible.

Coaches who wisely develop their ability to be flexible experience more success, not only in games, but interpersonally as well. For example, flexibility is a great tool to avoid head-on attacks when an athlete challenges you with harsh words or accusations. I've witnessed a superb college baseball coach resolve a conflict with one of his athletes by pausing, then looking for ways to go around, over, or under the conflict to get at the heart of the issue. He confronted the problem by listening to and absorbing the comments, and the conflict began to fade. In this situation, soft was strong, and the athlete realized his unreasonableness and apologized for being disrespectful.

Remember that your goal as a creative, effective coach is to protect, not destroy, the athlete's spirit and sense of self. You need not compete with an athlete; flexibility and humor are effective tools for resolving conflict. By going head-to-head you run the risk of creating negative, harsh environments in which athletes will resent you and sabotage your efforts.

One creative high school track and field coach had a rule of thumb about any disgruntled athlete who flew off the handle: When anyone vented frustration in the form of an attack, the coach asked that the attacker continue the barrage, uninterrupted, for 10 minutes. When the time was up, the frustration was eased, the attack had disappeared, the attacker got softer, and the coach had 10 minutes to compose his response. Being listened to in this fashion enabled his athletes to maintain their dignity, respect, and sense of self. The coach, obviously, felt strong and secure enough to handle these situations in this manner. This approach creates an open, two-way learning experience for coach and athlete alike.

The martial art aikido teaches how to defeat an opponent by being flexible and blending with the opposing force. When Vince Stroth, former offensive guard with the NFL's Houston Oilers, wanted a more effective way to derail his opposing lineman, I taught him this powerful principle of blending with the force of his opponent. Vince began to step to the side and take the lineman down with little effort using the force of that lineman to his own advantage. Vince learned that by being flexible and blending with extreme force, you can triumph without too much fighting.

Look for ways to help your athletes be adaptable and be victorious in the process. For example, if you believe that your athletes have the potential for great performances, tell them so; instruct them to relax and to do what they know to do and to be how they want to be. There's no need to force it or *make* it happen. Encourage them to let the game or performance come to them; to yield and let it happen. Remind them that if they do what they know they can do, good things will happen. Encourage athletes to trust the body's innate wisdom, developed by years of training in sport.

In a relaxed state, with your eyes closed, imagine an athlete coming at you with a verbal barrage. Notice how upset she feels. Feel the intensity. Probably your usual immediate response would be to attack back: "I'll show her, she can't talk to me like that." Instead, deflect the attack by being open to it, rather than tensing your body to shield yourself from the attack. Feel the sense of power; you are not being controlled by another. In a calm manner, express your feelings about being attacked and invite that person to talk more, to get it all out. Listen. Then, see yourself responding and making your points clearly, in a calm yet firm manner. Know that you have maintained your integrity and the athlete's dignity. I know this is contrary to instinct, but try this more flexible, open approach to conflict and see what happens. It may be difficult to respond this way all the time, but the more success you experience with it, the more often you will choose this route.

While the flexible, creative coach is like the willow tree, bending under forceful winds, the authoritative, rigid coach is like the stiff pine tree whose branches crack and break under pressure. Unreceptive to learning and to finding better ways to do things, the rigid coach ultimately feels the stress of forcing and pushing the athletes to accept one way as if it's the only or best way. Athletes tend to sabotage the efforts of unreasonable coaches by leaving the program or displaying inconsistent patterns of play. I believe that more than a few athletes failed to reach their potential under the leadership of former Indiana University men's basketball coach Bobby Knight, an authoritative coach, albeit a basketball genius.

Successful coaches and teams adapt to situations and therefore play better, improve, and learn.

Consider the work of coach John Wooden. He had authoritative tendencies, but because he treated his players fairly and as men, they respected him and played their hearts out. He was firm yet fair. When Bill Walton showed up one day to practice with a beard, he told Coach Wooden with strong conviction, "It's my right." Wooden replied, "I admire athletes who have strong beliefs and stick by them, I really do. We're going to miss you." Walton shaved the beard immediately. When you played for John Wooden, you played by his rules—out of love and respect for a man who demonstrated impeccable character. Profanity, disrespect, and abuse had no place in his system. His loyalty to one way, although rigid in some respects, was actually a loyalty to deeply rooted ethical concepts and basic good moral character. Because of this, his athletes could handle rules that may have seemed ridiculous to them.

Resolve Conflicts Fairly

Successful coaches know that many problems can be resolved without sacrificing or compromising their principles. However, a coach needs to be more flexible on issues that do not involve deeply rooted standards. Consider the example of a coach who wants a team to practice every day in the preseason, believing that this is the only sure path to creating toughness and endurance for the upcoming season. However, the athletes are on edge—tired, irritable, borderline injured, and becoming ill—and ask the coach for a day off. The coach immediately refuses, thinking they are too soft. Because of their insistence, he begins to listen and offers a fair compromise, which they agree to. He has them give one more hard effort, then follows that with a free day. The athletes come back charged up and ready to continue a vigorous regimen. In this case, the coach got what he needed, and the athletes respected him for listening to their concerns and for working to resolve the issue fairly (and flexibly, I might add).

However, there are some standards rooted in ethical concerns such as dependability, reliability, commitment to excellence, trustworthiness, teamwork, and integrity, to name a few, that will be nonnegotiable. For example, coming to practice on time every day with a strong commitment to work hard, trusting that the coach knows what's best, and supporting and encouraging the team are standards set by the staff that must be in place and must not be tampered with. By preserving these foundational standards, you become a strong, effective leader. Athletes will see that you are willing to listen and that you do not simply dictate rules. They will respect you for making a decision and sticking by it for the sake of the team's mission. Through your consistent, ethical behavior you inspire and guide athletes to higher levels of performance on and off the court. This requires you to be honest with yourself and to do what reasonable people would agree is the right thing. When you do, things go your way.

Coaching with outstanding character will likely require making unpopular decisions or even sacrificing wins to do what's right. If your star athlete fails to respect curfew, the best choice for the team may be to bench the athlete for a game, even at the risk of losing to an archrival.

Although being adaptable and open is indicative of leading fairly, I want to reiterate that the coach is, indeed, the primary decision-maker in all matters. Therefore the creative coach should not forget the importance of fairness—the quality of giving to athletes what they earn and deserve—in building strong team cohesion.

Treating athletes according to their abilities, status, and achievements is not fair to all athletes. Obviously, biases and prejudices related to ethnicity, gender, and religion must be eliminated. Yet this doesn't mean that everyone is treated exactly the same. For example, one athlete may be more dependable and willing to go all-out in practice, while another displays erratic patterns by showing up late or even missing a session from time to time. One athlete may consistently cause turmoil, while others adhere to the system.

Being fair does not necessarily mean that all athletes are given the same privileges. Some may have demonstrated their ability to handle more responsibility.

What, then, is fair? That is, how does a coach decide what will not be tolerated and what's acceptable? Sometimes coaches get caught off guard and handle a situation unfairly. For example, a star high school soccer player once had a tantrum during a practice, loudly cursing at his teammates because he got roughed up on one play. He stormed off the field and didn't return for the rest of practice. His team was shocked, yet the coaches did not say a word, even though this behavior was clearly contrary to team rules. When Saturday came, this athlete started in his usual position on the wing. The players were visibly upset because he had gotten away with unacceptable behavior and violating the team ethic. It wasn't fair that the incident had gone "unnoticed" by the coaches, that they had failed to reprimand him for his outburst and had instead rewarded him with a starting role.

When I saw this, I approached the head coach after the game and explained my concern. To his credit, he admitted his error; he had felt pressure to have his star playing in a big game. We talked about the message he was sending to the entire team and the problems that could cause. He called a meeting with his team and openly discussed his desire to rectify the situation. (We'll talk more about these issues when we discuss rule setting in chapter 5.)

We all make mistakes like this, and it's never too late to correct them. Athletes will appreciate your sincere efforts to make things fair by firmly adhering to team rules and staff expectations. Speaking of rules, one creative approach to rule setting is to sit down with the team before the season to talk about establishing rules that are fair, and to have all members involved in and responsible for their enforcement. Of course, coaches should have the final word when it comes to rules, particularly if they run contrary to the program's objectives.

Effective coaches remember that it is fair to be firm; it's not a form of punishment or discipline. Athletes are aware of this, too. Once rules and regulations are understood, a good coach will exhibit fairness by firmly enforcing the law. Athletes will feel more secure and be more compliant if there are clear boundaries. They will be better able to make wise choices because they'll know upfront what is expected and what will be tolerated, as well as the consequences of their actions for themselves and for the team. When upholding team rules, be sure to let the athletes know that it's not personal, that you still accept them but cannot tolerate a particular behavior. Point out that by being firm you are also being fair and are providing them with the opportunity for personal growth. To do this properly, let go of the need to be liked by your athletes; paradoxically, by doing so you will gain their trust and respect, and will be well liked and appreciated.

Fairness, therefore, is not capricious or variable. Athletes of high standing and recognition are not given special dispensation or privileges. Those of lower recognition are not treated more severely. Athletes who behave contrary to rules and expectations, even if they have a previously impeccable record, should still be treated with firmness. In all situations, have all athletes take responsibility for their behavior. Reward diligent, consistent, hard work toward a common goal. Be firm in holding to these standards. This is fair.

Coaching a team is sometimes like weeding a garden; you need to get rid of the weeds that are choking out the plants you're attempting to grow. Athletes who "do their own thing" are potential problems. Getting rid of athletes who are harmful to your program is not easy, but it is the fairest thing to do for the team in certain circumstances, especially if their mere presence could destroy what you've planted. A coach I work with at a major Division I university approached me about her star goalie. The team, ranked number two in the nation, needed this athlete if they were to contend for the national championship. Because of this, everyone put up with her obnoxious, disrespectful, hurtful behaviors; sulking when things didn't go her way and yelling inappropriate comments to her teammates during a game were commonplace. This began to take its toll on team morale and performance. The athletes became negative in their attitudes and unfocused in practice. Complaining and blaming became their modus operandi.

The courageous coach looked at her options and decided to give the athlete an ultimatum: Change the obnoxious patterns and be kind to your teammates, or cease to be a part of the team. The coach was firm in her message, even though she knew it could mean the end of a good season. The athlete took the choice to heart and decided to make the necessary changes. She apologized to everyone and promised to display good behavior. The team members became excited and embraced the "new" goalie for her efforts; they all got back on track and demonstrated stellar performance on their way to winning a national championship.

Athletes feel secure with clear, concise boundaries. They are more willing to comply and make better choices when they are held accountable.

It was a close call, but thanks to a creative, fair, and firm coach, change was possible for the athlete. Had she not been willing to change, relieving the team of the negative effects of her behavior would have been the best choice for the team and its future success. Sometimes you must be willing to lose in order to be fair. This is not easy, but the alternative is very damaging. Being firm and fair is the higher road to take, even if it means jeopardizing a season. On some level, do we not believe that coaching athletes is really about creating an environment in which they can become better people? Fairness is a lifelong quality, and in the long run, athletes will respect your no-nonsense approach and will know what the expectations are for them as well.

There are three simple rules of thumb to use when deciding whether your leadership is fair.

1. Treat others as you would like to be treated; the Golden Rule is fair and firm.

2. Be open to listening to the opinions of others when faced with decisions of fairness. Ask an athlete, "If you were the coach in this situation, how would you handle it?" You might even ask all the athletes in a team meeting what they

think would be fair under the circumstances. They often think of the fairest solution and come to realize the challenge you are faced with. You still decide how to best use those solutions.

3. Under no circumstances use force. You may win the battle, but you will surely lose the war. Talk firmly and stick to the boundaries; most athletes will conform to the rules.

Keep Your Cool

There's a lot of pressure being a coach. It's easy to become distracted and get off track when you are being judged by results. It takes strength of character and integrity to stay focused on your purpose. As coaches, you are not only developing athletes for the team's season or career, but you are also developing people for the future; it's really about teaching, and it is difficult to teach character to athletes if your character is compromised in an unrestrained pursuit of victory.

Winning is obviously important to all of us. Yet there are so many gauges by which we can measure success, and these should be emphasized as well: courage, tenacity, fearlessness, going all out, and the willingness to do what it takes to play your best. It takes solid character to be able to see victory other than on a scoreboard. It takes strength to face defeat when others around you see the team as a failure. If you keep your cool, stand behind your athletes' efforts, and keep them focused on the direction they should go, the journey will be positive. In time, they will reach heights they never thought possible.

Jack Elway, onetime coach at Stanford University, was asked by a reporter, "How does it feel to have a winning team after all these years?" His reply: "They have always been winners—it just didn't show on the scoreboard." Elway demonstrated strong character by not being persuaded by the media to think that because they hadn't won games they were losers. Sometimes coaching creatively involves learning to use your cognitive ability to respond on a level above the emotions of the game. Elway could have flown off the handle in response to the reporter's question, but instead he used a more cerebral, rational approach to defend his team with humor.

Many coaches have the ability to get to the top of their professions, to become champions—but without a strong sense of character, it will be difficult for them to remain in that position. As a coach, you are challenged with character issues every day; you need to find innovative ways to deal with those challenges. Find other individuals, if you can, who will offer support for your stance. But remember that you can't run a popularity contest. You will always meet with some opposition if you follow your heart and stick to what you intuitively know is right.

- I demonstrate a more humble approach when I provide my athletes with the positivity of the praise they deserve.
- When I accept what I've been dealt, I coach more effectively and increase the likelihood of success.
- I blend and bend rather than fight with might. With nonforce, I am truly the boss.
- I am a strong leader capable of being both firm and fair at the same time. When I am firm and fair, my athletes show a great deal of respect for and trust in my decisions.
- I refuse to give any person or situation permission to distract me from my character, who I am, and the ethics I hold to be true.

As you can see, the cultivation of strong character is the foundation of becoming an effective, creative coach. Without core ethical qualities, you run the risk of tearing yourself down instead of building your team up. Use strong character to create a solid team bond and an environment in which greatness and success can flourish. Such an environment will be greatly enhanced by the use of effective communication skills that will enable you to develop quality relationships with your athletes.

2

Communicating Effectively

Good communication is the essence of good coaching.

The most important and challenging skill for building strong relationships with athletes, staff, and others involved in your program is *communicating* effectively. Several successful coaches I work with tell me that good, productive communication is difficult, yet crucial to the essence of good coaching. For them, good communication fosters and instills confidence, courage, compassion, cooperation, and a sense of community in their athletes. Through good communication, these coaches learn as much from their athletes as the athletes do from them. The art of communication is essential, and it can be learned. The coach and team who communicate well, on and off the playing field, demonstrate the necessary maturity to get the job done.

Today's world of athletics is more challenging than ever. The pressures and demands you face as a coach are many. Athletes look for teams, programs, and schools that have coaches who can communicate to them with respect. For this reason, good communication starts with the recruiting process. When difficult situations arise on a team, as they certainly will, athletes expect to be treated as people; good communication between a coaching staff and team helps to build a trusting, safe environment, in which everyone can grow, with a focus on performing their best.

The pressures and demands of coaching are more easily addressed with effective communication. To meet this challenge you need to consider some creative ways to help you to communicate more effectively with athletes. Now, let's be realistic. There are hundreds of books about the development of effective communication skills. As a doctoral student in psychology, I had numerous courses in communication skills training. There is much to know about this specialty, yet you probably have a good head start on the subject just from what you've learned from daily interactions with your athletes, coaching staff, and administrators. In this chapter, I'll highlight some of the important aspects of communication to help you expand your skills and to become even more effective than you already are in relating to others. These aspects include the following:

- Listening
- Delivering your message
- Focusing on the positive
- Showing and earning respect
- Building and maintaining trust
- Showing compassion

Trying methodically to improve my communication skills for over 20 years has contributed to my success. Still, I admit that I don't always have the presence of mind to use these skills, especially if I become too emotionally invested in my cause. However, when I do use them, I'm always amazed at the outcome. The coaches we most admire and respect have developed similar techniques and have created very positive relationships with their athletes.

Good communication is the key to getting your point across and, as a result, to becoming more effective as a coach. It is crucial to remember to separate behaviors from the person; point out to athletes the behaviors or actions that they can improve rather than critiquing who they are as people. For example, you might say, "Kristin, I like the way you hustle, and I'm glad you're on the team, but your tardiness to practice has to go." Simply saying, "William, you're a great guy" will seem patronizing to an athlete if not tied to something more specific, such as, "I appreciate the way you give 100 percent effort when you are here. However, we need to look at why you frequently miss practice." By doing this, you minimize any potential defensiveness that might block communication.

Your objective, whether receiving or delivering a negative message, is to defuse anger and hostility and make the interaction less anxious and more receptive. Let's first consider how to facilitate communication when you are *receiving* a negative message.

Listening

To encourage effective communication, you must make yourself available for your athletes, creating a receptive and welcoming environment. When an athlete comes to you, simply hear him out; this sends the message that the person is valuable and deserves your time. Take his message seriously, even if it seems meaningless to you. Before the athlete says a word, try to establish an open attitude that you want to help and that you will accept his feelings even if you do not agree with them. (Don't confuse listening to an athlete with accepting what he is saying.)

Don't underestimate the value of further honing your listening skills. Listening is difficult, an art that takes patience and time to develop. Don't partially listen as you simultaneously prepare a counterattack—this does not give the athlete your full attention. To prevent yourself from doing this, ask yourself, *What is this athlete feeling right now?* Try genuinely to understand and empathize with her position. While she is talking, indicate that you are still listening via nodding or verbal cues, such as "I see" or "uh-huh."

Do not interrupt. This can be challenging, but it effectively ensures that a person has the chance to fully express himself. Hold on to what you want to say and express your feelings later. Write them down if you think you'll forget them.

To help refrain from interrupting, try using the skill of *reflective listening.* This is a strategy to indicate to the speaker that *I hear you* and *I understand what you've said.* You may reflect the content, or feelings, or both. For example, if an athlete complains to you, "Coach, I'm not getting enough playing time," you respond with, "So, you're wanting more minutes?" (reflecting content) or "You're not getting enough playing time and you feel [disappointed, cheated, upset]?" (reflecting content and feelings). Your statement should elicit a response, which you can continue to reflect until a resolution takes place. If your initial response to the athlete's concern or problem had been, "That's too bad, but you're not playing well enough right now to get more minutes," you would have shut down or seriously hindered communication. Chances are, the athlete's feelings of rejection would prevent her from confiding in you again. You would also run the risk of losing the athletes' trust in your leadership abilities.

Listen, listen, listen:the three keys to successful interaction. Reflect what you think the athlete is saying or feeling.

It's more constructive to wait until the athlete has spoken and then discuss, in a positive way, what can be done to address the concern. For example, say, "Now that we're clear on this, what do you suggest can be done to help us both get what we need?" Proceed to explore the viable options, giving your input along the way. The problem may not be completely resolved at the end of this conversation, but the athlete will walk away with a sense of dignity and self-worth. You will both be clear as to what step to take next toward resolving this issue, such as arranging a meeting to discuss or follow through with a plan.

Trust is another positive that can result from this process, and the athlete will have greater respect for you as a coach and person. Don't be afraid that you will lose control of a situation by listening to your athlete. In fact, by making the time to genuinely listen to the athlete, you will gain more control in the process of winning his trust and confidence. Moreover, you will help teach the athlete how to communicate and resolve problems constructively.

Delivering Your Message

Now, how about when you have a message to deliver, one that an athlete may not want to hear? For example, let's say one of your athletes has not been compliant with team preseason workouts. Everyone on the team is expected to run a two-mile loop, three days a week. Your star athlete has missed numerous runs, and when she does show up her lack of effort sends a negative message to her teammates (not to mention that her behavior has also hampered her conditioning). How do you and your coaching staff address this situation? You know that something needs to be done. After all, if the athlete isn't disciplined, the athletes on the team will see this as reflecting poorly on the coaches and the program. Would you call a team meeting and tell the athlete how she hurt her team and herself and threaten to discipline her if she didn't change? Would you call a meeting with just the coaches and the athlete to address the situation, or perhaps a one-on-one meeting in which one coach discusses the situation with the athlete?

Think about the possible outcomes for each option. In a team or three-on-one meeting, the athlete could become extremely defensive, feeling outnumbered by the coaches and powerless. This creates a no-win situation for all involved. If you were the athlete, what scenario would you feel best about? That scenario is the one that would be the best for resolving the situation.

I suggest that the head coach meet alone with the athlete and use a constructive communication method. One that I find effective is what I call the "I feel . . . when . . . because" method. You may start by saying, "I feel disappointed and frustrated when an athlete refuses to follow our program, because it shows lack of trust and destroys team spirit." You may, at this point, get more specific about the particular behavior if you sense that the athlete is not making the connection.

Such an approach keeps the lines of communication open, because it is personal and addresses the *behavior* of the athlete, rather than her *person;* it gives that athlete the opportunity to respond and be involved in the solution. It maintains the dignity of the athlete and lets the coach demonstrate assertiveness with less anger, hurt, and force—while giving the athlete the chance to think about the behaviors in question and future options.

After using the "I feel . . . when . . . because" method, listen to the response and, if the athlete accepts responsibility for her actions, ask, "How can you help me to solve this problem?" or "What can be done to resolve this?" This places the responsibility on the athlete. Perhaps the athlete will explain why she is behaving this way—she is overworked in her classes and burned out. She decides to drop a difficult course for now and focus on getting more rest. She promises to change her attitude and apologizes to the team and the staff.

Notice that this method does not use harsh, angry words that can destroy a relationship or can put an athlete on the defensive and thus interfere with honest communication. Though missing practices without good reason seems to be a pretty clear-cut reason for dismissal or benching of even a star player, the emphasis here is on resolving the problem in a productive way that gets athlete to first work to change her behavior and see how it ages the team rather than relying on the coach's obvious p to simply enforce punishment.

Avoid judgment, blame, put-downs, name-calling, and harsh threats—classic roadblock to effective communication.

I know, from using this approach, that it doesn't always duce an immediate resolution; an athlete may take it the wrong way and simply not cooperate. When this seems to fail (some athletes just don't respond to diplomacy), be direct, honest, positive, and low-key. Hostility will not work, ever. Try not to place extra emphasis on certain words. For example, instead of *"You must stop missing the run,"* try emphasizing to the athlete the positive results she'll experience by adhering to your system. For example, "When athletes consistently attend the running sessions, they *dramatically improve* their fitness level." Watch out for buzzwords that can trigger aggressive behavior. Avoid phrases such as "What were you thinking?" "How could you . . . ?" and "Why didn't you . . . ?" These are words that threaten others on a personal level. Remember, the attempt to communicate is half the battle. An appropriate pat on the back, or a hand on the arm, of an athlete is a powerful nonverbal communication that shows caring, sincerity, and concern.

Other staff, parents, officials, administrators—anyone who wishes to communicate effectively should give these skills a chance. Practicing on a daily basis will help you to master these skills.

Focusing on the Positive

Enthusiasm in your coaching is not simply passion and inspiration. It also manifests itself as exuberance, excitement, joy, courage, fearlessness, selflessness, and passion—qualities that create in each of us the drive, motivation, and ability to perform our very best.

Yet enthusiasm—as important as it is—cannot be legislated by anyone; it must be cultivated each day as a genuine by-product of your clear purpose or mission. Coaches, athletes, managers, and trainers need to understand that they, too, play a role in spreading this enthusiasm to anyone who comes in contact with the team. I suggest writing affirmations that reinforce this attitude on a piece of paper that is distributed to the team or posted in coaches' offices or locker rooms. The message can be this: "We refuse to give anyone permission to take away our enthusiasm." By zoning in on your purpose (see chapter 1, page 10), you create the opportunity for your athletes to tell you what excites them about achieving this goal and what they are willing to do to reach this higher level. If you are clear and vocal about your purpose—your personal vision and mission—you and your athletes will be better prepared to sustain motivation and perseverance throughout the season with great energy and enthusiasm.

I distinguish between genuine *enthusiasm of purpose*—a positive motivator—and *overzealousness*—a dangerous deceiver. An overly exuberant coach who rides on emotion is destined to lose his team when the inevitable slump hits. Teams and individuals seldom, if ever, win strictly on emotion, and even those who do are susceptible to inconsistent performance. Enthusiasm is a steady, inner sense of excitement, joy, and passion, rather than an external, emotional "rah-rah" kind of outburst that comes and goes.

Remember the story in chapter 1 about the head coach at Stanford University who told his staff and athletes that when things are going so well, they should all be on the lookout for problems? Negativity breeds bad feelings and douses enthusiasm for everyone in a program. Coaches and athletes become cautious, tight, and tentative—and, as in the case of the Stanford team, can sabotage their prospects of attaining their mission. Had this coach focused more on the positive, he could have freed his athletes to enjoy and take the risks necessary to achieve their goals. *Cautious optimism* enables you to enjoy and even celebrate your present achievements and to envision more of the same for the future, knowing that you will be ready to act on any changes that could take you off track. If you shoot for the moon, you will be farther along than if you hadn't tried, even if you fall short. No one has ever died from disappointment, but remorse (not "going for it") can be devastating.

Focusing on the positive does not mean you shouldn't constructively critique athletes to aid in their improvement or handle behavior problems effectively. I don't recommend that coaches sugarcoat feedback—that is, only tell athletes what they are doing well in practices and competitions. This is not what coaching is about. However, there are ways to teach athletes what and why they need to improve *constructively,* as opposed to creating a humiliating situation or giving only negative, failure-related feedback.

I once heard a high school basketball coach use sarcasm with a player who missed his first five shots in a game. He sat the athlete down and told him, "Pass the ball, don't shoot. You should give that shot to your grandmother." Although the player was playing quite effectively on the defensive side of the ball, the coach never mentioned this positive aspect of his play on the court. After the coach's comment, the athlete did not take a shot for the rest of the game. The enthusiasm this athlete had before the game was drained. The coach had an opportunity to tell the athlete how he could improve his shooting, but instead reminded the athlete what he did wrong. He could have taken the kid aside and said, "Matt, you're a great shooter; you just need to be sure you have an open shot before committing to it and taking it. By the way, good defense." This kind of interaction would keep enthusiasm burning for any player.

Bob Hansen, coach of the four-time national champion tennis team at the University of California, Santa Cruz, critiques in creative, positive ways, maintaining the dignity of his athletes and helping them focus on improving rather than dwelling on what is wrong with their playing. For example, Bob might say, "Jon, your strategy is superb. If you want to be even more effective, go to the net more often." Such a comment offers praise and tells the athlete how to be better at the same time. Quin Snyder, head men's basketball coach at Missouri, likes to coach players into improving on the court by making strong comments such as, "I love when you fight for position like that—now try not to reach in to get the ball, and you've got it." Quin's approach is a bit more revealing of his own feelings than Bob's, but both refuse to be hypercritical in their teaching. They are constructive in making comments intended to point out to a player what and how he can improve. By communicating needed improvements in this way, a coach can sustain and encourage enthusiasm and stay positive while improving player performance. Both Quin and Bob are *teachers* on the court, something all coaches should strive to be.

Catch your athletes doing what's right.
Give well-deserved compliments, but don't patronize.

Try some of these other ways to keep positive energy and enthusiasm flowing in the way you communicate with anyone involved in your program.

• Focus on an athlete's effort rather than results. Paul Wardlaw, tennis coach at the University of Iowa, reinforces his athletes for making the effort to prepare for a match and for playing with their best effort. This works especially well with athletes who get less attention than the stars. Choose athletes of the day or week and take time to point out the good they do and how you value their presence on the team. Encouraging an athlete's efforts (and correcting flawed technique in doing so) leads to better results.

• Do not resort to sarcasm and negative comments—especially with younger athletes, who tend to be more sensitive to them. Sarcasm and negativity extinguish the flames of enthusiasm. They inhibit an athlete's natural desire to take the risks necessary to improve.

- Earn respect by being fair and consistent in communicating to athletes. Give an athlete a safe, trusting environment. She will respect you and enthusiastically "go the distance."

- Demonstrate concern for your athletes in the way you communicate with them. For example, take an interest in one athlete's home life, then call to see how another one is feeling after a rough game or competition. Find one positive thing to say to each athlete during practice.

- Rather than tell an athlete what you don't want, express what you *do* want. For example, notice the difference between "Don't ever get in front of your opponent" and "Stay between your opponent and the basket." The latter is more constructive and positive and reinforces for the athlete what to do to improve (rather than what *not* to do).

- Be sure that your intention is clearly understood and realistically achievable. It's difficult to build enthusiasm in your coaching or in your athletes if the mission is vague or unattainable.

- Let your selflessness generate enthusiasm for yourself and others. Small but significant acts of caring and kindness create an environment in which enthusiasm can thrive: smile more often; tell someone how you appreciate his efforts; ask another how his day is going; plan a party in the team's honor; plan a special awards night, recognizing each athlete for individual efforts.

- When something terrific happens, be demonstrably positive about it.

- During difficult times, ignite enthusiasm by conducting team meetings to display strength, support, and encouragement. Talking about the difficulties can help to restore confidence in the team-as-family concept. A strong bond will help all to recapture their enthusiasm.

Coaches daily face many pressures and demands, weighed down by excessive paperwork and politics. I often hear this: "If I could only *coach*." At the high school level, coaches' salaries are meager and their responsibilities outside of coaching are enormous. In such pressured times, being positive and enthusiastic is all the more important in helping athletes, other coaches, and staff stay focused on and moving toward the mission at hand.

Enthusiasm is a habit that, like physical conditioning, comes with practice.

Keep in mind that to sustain enthusiasm, you must truly love what you are doing; your heart and soul must be into it. If not, you'll never experience real success. When you feel your enthusiasm fade, remind yourself of the opportunity you've been given to work with athletes and coaches and to have a positive impact on many people. Talk to other coaches who can give you a new perspective. Or pick up books written about coaches you admire or want to learn about. Learn how they approach their profession and maintain their enthusiasm.

Some of the best coaches reignite their love for sport by changing their approach and getting out of the rut; creating new, more meaningful objectives; and focusing more on their athletes as individuals. There will come a time, however, when you may need to consider the option of leaving coaching. Chronic low enthusiasm can be an indication that you need to move on. Before he retired, Dean Smith said that if ever a September rolled around and he felt he had lost his enthusiasm for the game, he would end his coaching career. He stuck to his words and left the game with dignity.

Showing and Earning Respect

It is only too often that we hear examples of athletes and coaches who, in an emotional pursuit of victory, engage in behaviors that are disrespectful and harmful to others. NBA player Latrell Sprewell attacked and choked P. J. Carlesimo, then his coach with the Golden State Warriors. Baseball player Roberto Alomar became infamous when he spit on an umpire. And not all acts of disrespect are a result of frustration or grudges. Some can result from jubilation, such as the 1999 U.S. Ryder Cup team's charging the green to celebrate Justin Leonard's putt while José Maria Olazabal had yet to finish the hole. Again, it's important to stay focused on the importance of establishing respect among your team, your staff, and even your opponents.

True respect is earned by the consistent display of solid, ethical character, not by a title or position. The key is to consistently respect others as you would like to be respected. This is not rocket science. It's this law of nature that, when observed, creates solid, respectful relationships among people without regard to title or position.

Good communication is the glue that binds a team, and respect is the foundation of all strong relationships. Your real strength and influence as a coach lie in relating to your athletes and staff with respect for what makes them who they are. You may have noticed that when an athlete is treated with disrespect, she often responds with resistance and resentment. On the surface, an athlete may comply with the wishes of the coach but will inwardly plot "revenge" through passive-aggressive behaviors such as tardiness, indifference, absenteeism, obstinacy, sulking, halfhearted effort, and other forms of counterforce. You may win the battle, but you lose the war.

Respect is the foundation of all strong relationships. Success is nonexistent without it.

Bill Bradley, in *Values of the Game,* said that the way a coach earns respect can vary from coach to coach. Hank Iba, his Olympic coach, garnered respect because of his thoroughness in practice. During practice, Iba used a blackboard to display diagrams for the offense, and athletes had to keep notebooks of these lectures. His attention to detail was always apparent. Bradley's coach at Princeton, Butch van Breda Kolff, gained respect because of his intensity in competition rather than his detailed structure. Van Breda Kolff coached more extemporaneously, with fewer set plays and a freelance offense in which players developed the ability to create in the moment of play. Their coaching styles and personalities were different, but both men received respect.

The Associated Press recently disclosed that two major university athletic programs had replaced head coaches after players boycotted practice, complaining that the coaches were disrespectful. Another coach resigned at a different university because the athletes accused him of verbal abuse. In addressing the issue of disrespect and verbal abuse, Wake Forest president Thomas Hearn stated that if he were to abuse students verbally, humiliate them, or call them names, he would be summarily fired—and rightly so. He affirmed that coaches should be held to the same standard.

Unfortunately, such incidents of disrespect are common in all levels of athletics, from youth leagues to the pros; they go unreported for the most part, and in some cases a slap on the wrist is the only intervention. What message does an administration send to its athletes and coaches in such cases? That disrespect is acceptable?

A few years ago I was working with a talented distance runner whose stellar performance at a major track meet qualified him for the Division I NCAA championships in the 10,000-meter run. This was quite an achievement, one deserving of respect from staff and fellow teammates. It was considered the top level of excellence for this sport. His diligent physical and mental efforts were being rewarded.

He ran one more race before the nationals and, with little incentive to race all out since the championship was just a few days away, used it simply as a good workout leading up to the "big one." Naturally, his time was below his best, but his coach was furious. The athlete tried to explain his tactic to the coach, but the coach jumped all over him and decided to prohibit his star from going to the championships, saying that he was afraid the athlete would embarrass his program. There was an obvious breakdown in communication between the athlete and coach, and perhaps a lack of respect on the part of both parties. The coach refused to listen to the athlete's reasoning and the athlete had failed to communicate his intention before the race. Both the young athlete and the coach were hurt by a mutual lack of respect. The athlete lost the chance to go to nationals, and the coach lost the chance to have a national champion—all due to disrespect and poor communication.

A good coach understands the need for mutual respect and the impact it has on high-level performance. You may have noticed that when you treat athletes with respect, they are more willing to give it their all. Also, when coaches respect athletes, it creates a spirit of loyalty. We witness it all the time: athletes who feel respected take on more hardship, suffering, and sacrifice for the sake of attaining the team's mission.

Bill Walsh, successful past head football coach of the San Francisco 49ers and Stanford University, is considered by many to be an honest, respectful leader. He was absolutely straight with his athletes. He rarely, if ever, lashed out at anyone, and still won the big games. This is not to say that raising your voice is, in itself,

The mutual respect and honest communication between coach Bill Walsh and his players resulted in success for Stanford and for the 49ers.

detrimental, but your words must not diminish the integrity and dignity of the athlete.

Another coach who exhibits a great deal of respect for his athletes is Quin Snyder, men's basketball coach at the University of Missouri. Like Walsh, Coach Snyder develops athletes into quality players and quality people. His respect for his athletes is matched only by the respect they shower on him. Quin is a coach with a warrior's spirit (to fight hard to win) and a teacher's heart (to assist his players in continuing their athletic and personal growth). He is able to reprimand an athlete with dignity and respect, and as a result the athlete invariably accepts the responsibility for his own behavior.

In Quin's first season as head coach, one of his star players mouthed off during a practice, almost as if to test his new coach.

The player's frustration was apparent, but his approach was unacceptable. Rather than react from his ego and chastise the athlete in front of his teammates, Quin went silent, looked at the player for 10 seconds (which seemed like an eternity to everyone on the court), and then resumed play. After practice, Quin and this player met face-to-face. Coach Snyder talked to this young man, telling him, "I understand your frustration, but I will not tolerate such outbursts." With tears of regret, the athlete apologized. Through respect for the athlete and the team, Quin demonstrated to the player and everyone on the court his strength, control, and focus that day. The team's respect for their rookie coach grew immensely.

*Mutual respect is essential for
high-level performance.
Winning is difficult, inconsistent, and volatile
in disrespectful environments.*

When asked about the Boston Celtics' secret of success, former coach of the NBA champions Red Auerbach simply stated, "We treated them [the players] with respect." Bob Hansen, coach of four-time national tennis champions University of California, Santa Cruz, wins because he gets more out of athletes through unconditional respect. His athletes tell me that they'd do anything for Bob because he shows them so much respect as athletes and as people. They, in turn, have great respect for him.

Here are some ways that Bob communicates his respect for his athletes through the course of the season:

- He solicits their opinions about training and acts on them. For example, Bob might ask, "We need more endurance; we seem tired when we should have energy. What do we need to do?"
- He includes them in the formulation of team rules and policies, such as curfew on road trips.
- He is a man of his word, never saying one thing but doing another. If he tells the team they can have a day off if they practice with passion, he follows through.
- He listens to athletes' gripes with an open heart and acts on them if appropriate.

These are some basic guidelines you can put into practice when you wish to extend your respect to your athletes. This is also another way for you to solicit feedback on your coaching from your athletes and other coaches. Great respect, once again, comes from open communication.

Many of you may be assistant or associate coaches who act as mediator between the head coach and athletes. An athlete might go to you for advice because she does not necessarily want to talk to the head coach directly. This can become a delicate situation; there is a very fine line between being respected by an athlete and being a friend to the athlete. Young coaches who relate well to their athletes because of their age often find themselves in this situation. To keep things straight, the principles and strategies that ring true for the head coach relate to you as well. There is no need to impress others; you simply need to give them the respect they deserve. The concept of respect is universal. Whether you're the head or assistant coach, treat others as you would expect to be treated, and they will likely reciprocate.

Respect for others begins with respect for yourself.

Any coach who wants to respect others must nurture self-respect by using the basic character qualities discussed in chapter 1 when a decision needs to be made. "As it is within, so it is without"; to be a respectful leader, teach through your own example. Know, however, that we are all human beings. We do get off track. If you slip on the respect issue, what matters is how quickly you can come around. A simple "I'm sorry, my emotions ran away from me" can go a long way in reestablishing trust and respect.

Help your athletes to see that sport is all about respectful relationships. Encourage them not to be hard on themselves in defeat or injury. Expect teammates to show respect for one another by committing to push one another to greater heights in practice. Create a selfless *we, not me* environment in which all understand that the whole is greater than the sum of its parts. Demand that your teams respect opponents, treating them as partners in helping you reach your full potential and playing with all you have. Sport is a microcosmic classroom, a teacher for all of life, an opportunity to discover your innermost self. Mutual respect means that you are all in this together, wanting what's best for all involved. Without respect, strong relationships are nonexistent, making effective coaching an impossibility.

Building and Maintaining Trust

Trust in leadership is critical to team success. Kurt Dirks, an assistant professor of business administration at Simon Fraser University in Vancouver, British Columbia, questioned 355 athletes from 12 collegiate teams to gauge their level of trust in their coaches. He analyzed the trust results in relation to the teams' records, coaches' tenure, team talent, and other factors. In the end, only two factors had a significant effect on conference records—talent, followed closely by trust in the coach. The two teams that showed the greatest trust in their coaches turned out to be exceptionally successful national standouts. The team with the lowest levels of trust lost about 90 percent of their conference games.

Most reasonable people believe that coaches have athletes' best interests at heart, wanting team members to be happy, successful, and productive in their endeavors. Yet athletes do not perceive this to be true of all coaches at all times. Some athletes feel that their coaches are dishonest, unreliable, undependable, and unfair—in a word, untrustworthy. In the same way, athletes may prove untrustworthy to coaches. Trust is a two-way street, and all parties involved are responsible when a breakdown occurs. Again, if trust falls by the wayside, coaches and athletes need to rely on communication skills to reestablish contact to resolve the issue.

Trust flourishes in environments with
good communication, respect, and nurturing.

During a recent visit to one of the university athletic programs I work with, I was approached by numerous athletes disgruntled with the coaching staff for not being honest, fair, and "straight" with them. They told me how the staff would say one thing, yet do another, promising, for example, "If you play hard in practice, you'll get a day off tomorrow," then not delivering the promised payoff when the athletes gave it their all. Trust between players and coaching staff was lacking, and the team's inconsistent and erratic performance reflected this. The players appeared to give up in tight games because they didn't care; they stopped giving their best effort in practices because they didn't trust that the coaches knew how to train them correctly. They told me that the coaches contradicted one another and thus they weren't sure which coach to believe. Without this trust, the team was unwilling to give it their all; morale dipped as they blamed one another or external factors for their poor performance. There was a "trust meltdown" as the coaches, in turn, began to distrust the athletes. The program was in dire need of attention.

I called a meeting with the staff to share what I observed to be a virus spreading through the ranks, one that needed swift attention. I mentioned that the athletes did not necessarily want to have anything special; they simply needed the coaches to be honest and to communicate more directly with them. The coaches knew something was not right but didn't realize the role they played in the problem. I pointed out that the problem was an interaction, and that both they and the athletes were the cause.

To the coaches' credit, they accepted their part and called a team meeting. The coaches listened to the athletes' gripes, then voiced their own concerns. The staff solicited the athletes' input on positive directions and change. They listened to the athletes' suggestions and made plans for implementing new approaches. The athletes specified their need for the staff to communicate clearly to them and to follow through on what was promised. The coaching staff decided to hold bimonthly meetings to check in and make sure everyone was on the same page. The coaches worked on improving their communication, and the athletes did their part by following the directives set down by the coaches. Getting everything out on the table was a big part of the solution.

Of course, sometimes distrust can be spawned by one or two "bad apples"—athletes who only want to be negative and see the coach or the program fail. Just as a gardener removes weeds that are choking the healthy plants, you should get rid of negative forces that threaten the health of your team. But first, approach the distrusting parties. Discuss with them what you observe to be a "virus" that is infecting the team. Provide them with a positive solution to let them change their direction, and clarify the one alternative—to leave the team. Even if these athletes are the stars of the team, their negativity and mistrust will hurt the whole team and erode team unity if you don't address the situation.

There are several creative ways you can build and maintain team trust. When heavy anger looms, have athletes and coaching staff write out their grievances on paper and hand them in anonymously. If the anger and mistrust have built up over a period of time, consider repeating this activity once a month to work incrementally at solving the problem. Conduct this activity any time you sense that tensions are particularly high. You may not like what they say, but if there is any truth to their statements, you can begin to make appropriate changes and build some trust. Read through these grievances with the other coaches and decide what can be done. Call a full team meeting to address all grievances filed and what the program will and will not change (and why). Work together to implement constructive change.

Involve athletes, when appropriate, in decision-making processes.

Keep in mind that athletes, when experiencing loss, injury, or troubled times, may mistakenly blame their misfortune or unhappiness on external factors—such as your coaching style or other issues with the program. They may point the finger at the system, not realizing that they too need to share some of the responsibility for the problem. In the example on page 49, it was clear that in spite of the athletes' misgivings about their coaches, they were not putting in the time and effort to succeed and were refusing to exert full effort in competition. A team not practicing or playing to its potential is not going to achieve its ultimate performance in competition. In this example, the coaches talked to the athletes about regaining a sense of self-respect and personal pride and playing for themselves, regardless of their feelings about the staff.

Immediately after these interactions, this team had one of their best competitive weekends of the season. However, the following week these athletes returned to their passionless, lackluster play, losing three matches to close rivals. What happened? The coaches hadn't followed through to address the real problem of mistrust and had not made the necessary changes. The athletes soon realized that the coaches' pep talk about the team pulling together had been lip service, which is another form of disrespect. If you say one thing and do another, trust will break down. Always ask the question *How can I establish trust in this situation?* and let the answer guide your actions and behavior.

Some athletes will bring baggage from other adult relationships that cause them to be distrustful. Perhaps the athlete found that one or both of their parents were untrustworthy, abusive, or neglectful. This can be difficult to ascertain during the recruiting process, but you can certainly ask recruits to describe their relationship with their parents. If you are patient, show good character, communicate openly, and don't let your own past interfere with the situation, the athletes will eventually drop the barriers as you continue to model trust. If problems persist after repeated attempts to rectify the situation, you can always consider parting ways as a solution. I recently worked with a team that experienced a severe breakdown in trust between an athlete and her coaching staff. There were too many philosophical differences and cultural gaps between them that were irreconcilable. The athlete, to her credit, decided to leave this program for another that was more aligned with her way of thinking.

As coaches, if we wish to be trusted, we must dare to trust those we lead. In the scenario described earlier, in which the trust between athletes and staff fell apart, the coaches temporarily reversed the downward spiral by demonstrating trust in their athletes' concerns. But the staff failed to continue the process, and things eventually began to fall apart again. It's important for coaches to continue to work on relationships, communicating and following through on their word consistently, not just reactively patching up crises when they occur.

Dare to trust those you lead
or move them toward earning your trust.

There are many ways to demonstrate your trust in others and therefore to earn their trust. Following are a few effective ways to develop a strong sense of mutual trust.

• Communicate with and show respect for your athletes and coaching staff.

• Search for ways to involve the team in the decision-making process. Decisions about dress code, curfew, and absenteeism are great topics for athletes to involve themselves in. When you demonstrate your trust in them to make good choices, they will trust you in return. Be sure to follow through on their input.

• Avoid looking over your athletes' shoulders after giving them a directive—give them the benefit of the doubt that it will be carried out. Micromanaging your athletes or coaches creates dependency and forces them to second-guess themselves, eroding their confidence that they can get the job done. Don't be afraid of losing control. Ironically, when you let go and check up less frequently, the athletes or other coaches will feel trusted and take the initiative to complete the task. If someone takes advantage of your trust and doesn't carry out the directive, communicate with that person that you are disappointed and that your trust has been violated. Ask the person what he thinks should be done to rectify the situation.

• Give athletes the room to make mistakes, and even to fail. Show them that mistakes are our teachers, and refuse to rush to their rescue when there's a setback. Be supportive and have an open-door policy for listening, allowing them to talk about their mistakes—but don't bail them out every time. They need to correct the situation and to demonstrate their eagerness to learn from failure.

• Practice what you preach; make your actions congruent with and reflective of your mission, what you intend to create. For example, there was a coach who demanded respect and trust of his athletes, yet didn't provide his assistants or other coaches in the department with the same trust or respect—at times even bad-mouthing the assistants in front of athletes. Such behavior runs contrary to what you wish to teach—mutual respect and trust. Consistency is key to establishing trust.

Be patient in winning your team's trust in your mission and in the purpose and direction of your program. If you have an established, successful program, it is easier for athletes to buy into the system. I see this with teams that have won league, conference, and national championships. They trust the way of the staff; they are relaxed, calm, and confident in the plan. However, it can be more difficult if you are a new coach in a program and have not established your track record. Without trust, players may be more tense and less willing to listen to what you have to say, which interferes with success. In such cases progress may seem slow, yet you must trust your dream. Remember that when you plant a garden, you do not pull up on the plants so they can grow taller and faster; you allow them to grow naturally. In the same way, you can't rush the natural process of earning trust. Trust is earned when you act according to your sound character and mission, being fair, honest, communicative, and dependable.

Practice what you preach.
Consistent action is the key to trust.

Learning when to trust others is a process that takes time. People will give you reasons to trust or distrust their behavior. If an assistant has a lack of trust for the orders of the head coach when she doesn't believe in the philosophy or directive, the two should sit down and try to get clear on matters. When in doubt, talk it out. Most problems that occur around the issue of trust are the result of a lack of communication. Talk things out before they get too out of line.

So it is with any team. Soccer coach Alan Kirkup experienced a difficult beginning when he took over the program at the University of Arkansas. Having been highly successful at Southern Methodist University, Alan knew it would take four to five years to build a winning program at Arkansas. However, the going was rougher than he thought it would be the first half of his initial season; it took time to undo some of the old, sloppy work habits from the previous year and for the team to begin to trust Alan's vision and methodology.

Alan, his staff, and I worked together, helping the athletes to commit to going all out with courage, fearlessness, tenacity, and selflessness, qualities necessary for championship levels of performance. We defined what each quality was and what each team member needed to do to demonstrate that quality, and then expected them to go out and do it. For example, we defined *courage* as the willingness to go for the 50/50 ball or to sprint back on defense; *fearlessness* was defined as the willingness to take a calculated risk and thereby increase the chances of being a better player. *Selflessness* was illustrated by the willingness to look for specific ways to serve the team and then to follow through on those ideas. It became a very task-oriented, pragmatic exercise in assisting this team to execute the intangibles.

As time went on, more and more athletes began to buy into this system, exhibit these qualities, and trust Alan's mission. As his plan began to take hold, the players started to pull it together and won five of their last six games. Trust in his system and in one another enabled them to turn around an otherwise lackluster season and begin to prepare with excitement for their next season.

We need to stop reaching for the measurements—scores, points, records, or outcomes—and trust that our programs are on the right track. We may be winners even if it's not reflected on the scoreboard. Do not abandon your trust in one another, even if things are temporarily unclear.

Showing Compassion

Compassion is that inner perspective that enables you to empathize with another, to look at a situation from that person's point of view. This is such a crucial quality in a coach, that teams (coaches and athletes alike) who possess it achieve great things.

Compassion creates cooperation
and helps to sustain high levels of excellence.

Phil Jackson claims that large doses of compassion, more than anything else, allowed the Bulls to sustain a high level of excellence over the years they dominated the NBA. Compassion means encouraging your athletes to accept one another in spite of differences. Compassion means accepting failure if it comes and focusing during setbacks on the effort rather than the outcome. When athletes are treated with compassion, they become more cooperative and loyal, their performance improves, and true winning becomes the natural by-product.

Coach John Thompson recognizes the value of coaching with compassion.

In 1982, Georgetown University was on the brink of winning the NCAA men's basketball championship. But in the championship game, as the final seconds ticked off the clock, GU guard Freddie Brown inexplicably threw the ball into the hands of North Carolina's James Worthy, spelling defeat for the Hoyas. Georgetown coach John Thompson sought out Brown after the buzzer sounded, not to scold him, but to offer words of encouragement as he escorted him off the court, an arm warmly slung around his dejected freshman guard's shoulders. Thompson explained that they would not have gotten to the title game without him.

Coach Thompson's overt demonstration of compassion reinforced to his team that mistakes happen and that we can learn from them. This approach allowed the GU athletes to play relaxed rather than becoming afraid of making a mistake. To win, we must be free to fail, to take the risks that will allow us to discover our greatness. Thompson created an environment of compassion in which athletes felt free to discover this greatness. And of course, in 1984, Freddie Brown and his teammates were able to surmount the obstacles they encountered two years earlier and climb all the way to the national title.

Coaches' compassionate acts are seldom as public or obvious as Thompson's was at the 1982 NCAA tournament, though the image of Bela Karolyi picking up injured gymnast Kerri Strug off the mat in the 1996 Olympics is equally prominent in the mind's eye. But these are only two examples of hundreds of such caring behaviors by coaches on all levels of sport, every day. Even small gestures that tell your athletes they're important can make all the difference in the world. Legendary high school cross country coach, Joe Newton, makes a point of saying something to each of his 100-plus athletes at practice each day, signaling to every single one of the teenagers that he appreciates their contribution to the team, no matter how big or small.

Compassionate acts by coaches are not limited to the court, track, or field. Many coaches give a great deal of their time, energy, and in some cases money to charitable causes, demonstrating a deep sense of caring for those less fortunate than them. Coaches Against Cancer, The Jimmy V Foundation, and a host of other causes are among the beneficiaries of coaches' compassionate side.

Even tough-as-nails baseball manager Tony LaRussa has a tender spot. The Animal Relief Fund that he developed in 1991 has helped find homes for thousands of animals who would otherwise likely succumb to starvation, disease, or animal control measures. Not only does ARF keep animals alive, it strives to match them with owners who will benefit at least as much from the arrangement as the animals do themselves.

Direct, personal demonstrations of compassion to players is best, but through other acts of giving, coaches reveal a level of concern for others that may not always be apparent within tightly run practices and intensely fought competitions. Such behaviors make athletes aware that there is a caring person in charge and help coaches keep connected with an essential part of their beings.

There are many ways to inspire compassion other than the overt method Coach Thompson used. Henry Bibby, coach of the USC basketball team, would use praise to show compassion. After a tough loss in a playoff game, he told the press, "We had victories you couldn't even see."

What does lack of compassion produce? We've all seen coaches severely chastise athletes for costly mistakes, even during a routine competition, sometimes even in front of the hometown fans. This lack of compassion often affects players, fans, and coaches alike. Perhaps you've noticed that an athlete often responds to such harsh words by competing or playing with fear of making a mistake. The athlete's tentativeness makes it difficult for him to take the risks necessary to improve. Coaches can help to lessen the fear by what they say and do—in particular, by apologizing for sudden outbursts (or learning to control them altogether). I have heard some coaches tell their athletes, "I may raise my voice at you from time to time. It's not a personal thing about you, it's just an expression of frustration in the heat of battle. My behavior is not indicative of how I value you." Such a reminder to a team or athlete can go far in establishing compassion.

Athletes who experience compassion
are more willing to go all-out, take risks,
and perform with reckless abandon.

Harry Groves, head track and field coach at Penn State, is a natural at showing his athletes compassion. When he encounters athletes who have a fear about competing, he uses positive comments as well as humor to alleviate prerace anxiety. I heard him say to an athlete before a race, "If you win, I'll love you, but if you don't [he hesitates for a few seconds to let the tension build] . . . I'll still love you, so get in there and have a good time—it's only a race." The athlete he said this to, a freshman, ran the race and recorded his fastest time ever for the distance. His comments reduced the pressure and communicated to the athlete that Harry understands the fear and anxiety that can come with competing, but that he believed in the athlete's ability to go out there and do it. Getting into the shoes of the athlete makes it easier for Harry to demonstrate his compassion. Having been a competitive runner, Harry has experienced prerace anxiety firsthand and realizes all the more that athletes need to lighten up and laugh to be fluid, smooth, and efficient while on the run. His compassion usually spills over to the entire team—they become compassionate with one another, forgiving one another and growing together through setbacks or tough times.

You might not have a style like Harry's, but you can show compassion in your own style. Just remember that there are two kinds of athletes: those who have failed and lost, and those who will. Having such compassion also helps you to be more humble in victory by recognizing how it feels to be on the losing side.

As a coach, you are in a perfect position to instill compassion in your athletes. Yet athletes can also benefit from being compassionate to one another. After an early-season loss to underdog University of Delaware, Maryland's field hockey team members were emotionally defeated and spiritually depleted. In search for the reason for the unexpected setback, they resorted to blame and finger-pointing. Some were extremely self-critical and felt the weight of the defeat. As a result, they began to play tentatively and fearfully, losing two consecutive games on the road.

The low morale called for a team meeting. The team talked about "heart" and compassion and discussed the ways they could pull together and share responsibility for their performance. They began to embrace the concept of compassion for themselves—individually and as a team—using forgiveness as a way to go forward after loss, setbacks, and failure. With trust, love, and compassion, they were able to open up their play, to go all out, take risks, and perform with reckless abandon.

After this crucial session, they went on a nine-game tear, including a 1-0 overtime victory against the University of Virginia to win the Atlantic Coast Conference (ACC) championship. Compassion for one another, according to head coach Missy Meharg, was the most significant ingredient in her team's excellent run because it allowed the women to pick themselves up from setbacks in games and go forward as a cohesive unit. As you can see, there is tremendous value to communicating effectively in all facets of sport.

Be able to forgive yourself.

Creative coaches take the time to show their athletes that they are concerned about their lives. They also encourage athletes to support and help one another when down, injured, or experiencing setback and loss. You can ask your players to take the time to imagine what it might feel like to be in a less fortunate person's shoes. Give compliments to athletes who feel like they don't measure up, but let your words be sincere or they'll see through them. Most of all, have compassion for yourself, a coach who works hard to create the best for all but who will also experience a share of struggle and setback. Self-compassion allows you to forge ahead when everything around you seems to be on the verge of collapse.

- I look for opportunities to be more available to my athletes. I set up times when they know I will be there for them.
- I consistently look for ways to demonstrate my passion and enthusiasm to others.
- I cultivate respect for our competitors, our game, and the team.
- When I treat others as I wish to be treated, I create healthy, productive, successful athletic environments. Soft is strong.
- When I demonstrate trust with my athletes, I create an environment of loyalty, respect, and encouragement. Trust is a must.
- I show concern, encourage support, and compliment sincerely.
- Creating competitive situations enables my athletes to risk, lose, and get better because of compassion.

Compassion has been the treasure and foundation of the most effective leaders worldwide for centuries. The ancient Chinese sage Lao-Tzu said that leaders whose positions endure are those who are the most compassionate; when two armies meet, the one with compassion is the one that tastes victory.

3

Creating an Atmosphere of Service

When you serve your athletes, you become more capable of leading them.

According to a Chinese proverb, to rule is to serve, and to serve is to rule. This is also true in coaching. By assuming a role of service with your athletes—being a good role model and offering them opportunities to realize their potential in a safe, nurturing environment—you become a more effective coach. Serving your athletes in this way affords them the freedom to take the risks necessary for growth and development. This, in turn, serves the best interests of the athletes and the team in achieving their potential.

By *serving,* I do not mean catering to every wish an athlete might have. The athletes are not in charge, and you do not need to win their approval by being compliant to their wishes and desires. Such catering is not service and does not help athletes grow and develop.

Some compare coaching to parenting in the sense that both take on the responsibility of serving in the personal development of young people. While parents and coaches have somewhat different interests in the young person, the efforts of both are reflected in the conduct and performance of those under their guidance. As a parent of athletic children, I lend my kids to a coach hoping that he will serve them the same care I would give in teaching them the skills of the sport as well as the sportsmanship, discipline, and conduct lessons that come with playing. Just as parents want to create a healthy home environment for their children, a coach also wants to serve by providing the best environment for athletes to reach their potential. Good coaches, like good parents or teachers, treat their athletes as individuals and with respect, kindness, and dignity. Athletes feel worthwhile and important in such environments and are willing to give back a hundredfold in effort.

Tim Gullikson provided a shining example of how to establish a positive, serving coach-player relationship before brain cancer tragically took his life at the young age of 44. Gully loved to coach, and thought he was born to become one. As a former overachieving pro player of modest abilities, he knew the athletes' side of the coach-player relationship.

Easily the most popular pupil of Gully's was Pete Sampras. The two hooked up in 1992, and in the four years they worked together before Gully's death, the coach made a lasting, positive impact on his star athlete's tennis career and outlook on life.

"I realized how vulnerable we all are," Sampras said in a June 1996 interview (New York AP, June 27, 1996). "Tim was 44, didn't abuse his body, was a good person, and was taken away from us. It made me do some soul-searching . . . . Tennis is a great game but ultimately it's going to end and it's not the most important thing in life. It kind of put everything in perspective."

These kinds of nurturing relationships are probably even more important in individual sports and in sports that emphasize individual events because these athletes don't get the general team support of other athletes. Also, training can be so much more individual and the coach gets to spend more time with each athlete. An excellent example of this is Bela Karolyi, controversial gymnastics coach of several Olympians. In many respects, he became a surrogate father for his athletes, who were away from their immediate families to train with him. Temple basketball coach John Chaney has spoken out against a system that can exploit athletes. He speaks about racism, money, entitlement, and other

Coaches who assume a role of service to their athletes will find that athletes reciprocate and strive to do their best.

issues that impact athletes. He acts as a protector of the best interest of his players, as individuals and as a team.

Successful coaches who model an attitude of service find that their athletes are more open to approaching their coaches for advice and guidance. The athletes give their best efforts on and off the field when they learn and train in an environment in which they can take risks and grow.

This chapter highlights some of the important cornerstones of service a coach provides to athletes: nurturance, encouragement, firmness with fairness, acceptance, affirmation, and time. You may be thinking, *I just don't have time to look for ways to serve my athletes; I'm busy enough with coaching.* Although creating ways to serve can take extra time, you will find out that you can creatively build service into the coaching tasks that you already do. By doing so, you will open up your athletes to reaching their highest potential, and athletes will return the service. In fact, you will find that you probably save time in the long run and in the progress of your athletes by creating an atmosphere of service.

Nurture and Encourage

Bob Hansen, who has coached the University of California, Santa Cruz, men's tennis team to four national championships, continually encourages his athletes' growth in sport and as young adults. He not only guides them in their on-court training and conditioning, but he also takes an interest in athletes' academics and home lives as well. By taking the time to check in on each athlete he stays aware of what is happening with them—when they have tests, if the family dog has just died, and so on. He works to keep communication open by taking the time to call his athletes at home or to invite them to his house. Bob's nurturance and guidance ignite the power of passion within his athletes—extraordinary motivation, excitement, enthusiasm, energy, joy, and love for sport and life. Naturally, Bob uses the principles of communication we talked about in chapter 2 to best serve his athletes, but he still needs to make the effort to seek out and talk with each athlete. Bob isn't crossing the boundaries and becoming a peer or friend of his athletes by taking this genuine interest in how they're doing. Rather, he takes this time as a given part of how he can best coach his athletes. His players have not had trouble deciphering this fine line.

Keep in mind that delving too deeply into an athlete's personal life could be a setup for trouble. Keep your calls to issues about athletics, and discuss appropriate personal issues only when initiated by the athlete. If the subject matter is beyond your expertise, guide the athlete in getting professional input from a competent sport psychologist, counselor, or other specialist.

Ask Questions

If you are looking for creative ways to serve through nurturing and encouraging, start by asking your athletes the following four questions:

1. What would it take for you to play at a higher level?
2. What would you like me to do to help you?
3. Are you feeling fulfilled in this program?
4. Is there some way the coaching staff or program could be more helpful?

These questions are best asked in a one-on-one meeting between the athlete and you. You and your staff can determine when an athlete is in need of such encouragement. Often, asking these questions before the start of a season is a good way to help athletes become focused on raising the bar.

During these one-on-one meetings, pay attention to your athlete's personal complaints and issues. Listen with respect. As you sift through the information that the athlete has provided in answering these questions, write the responses down. Discuss the issues with the staff to get their input on how to best address the athlete's needs. This is an excellent forum to help each athlete to better understand her role on the team. When question 4 is asked, an athlete may reply, "I'd just like to get more playing time, Coach." Your response might be, "I'd love to do that for you, and I will when I see your level of commitment rise. Here are the things you need to do if you want your role to expand. . . ." Specifically determine what the athlete needs to do to prove her level of commitment has improved. An athlete's response to these questions may require help from other resources. If so, find outside assistance, rather than going beyond your expertise. A competent, dedicated professional sport psychologist can help serve many athletes' mental and emotional needs.

You'll need to decide when an athlete needs a pat on the back as opposed to a "kick in the rear." This will become second nature as you take the time to really get to know your athletes and what motivates them. The four questions at the beginning of this section will be helpful in this regard. Patting an athlete on the back may not be the best thing to do in all situations. Don't be afraid to make a mistake! You will learn and become a better coach by taking risks and noting the outcomes. As a result you'll learn to decide which situations call for praise and which call for a firmer approach.

Be Firm, but Fair

An important corollary of nurturing and encouraging athletes by listening to their criticism is to remain firm. Weigh suggestions, but always hold on to your own values and clearly communicate the team's purpose. Otherwise you may confuse serving your athletes with being a slave to them. I know of a head coach at a major NCAA program who wanted to be liked so desperately that she would look for ways to please *all* the athletes, even if it required bending the rules to do so. For example, she was more lenient on tardiness and absence from practice with the star athletes than she was with others on the team. She began to tolerate fighting, yelling, and foul language from athletes she needed for game day. She became a slave to the changing whims of many of her athletes, and this leniency caused problems. Players started to interpret the bending of the rules as meaning that the rules didn't really matter, that they could do whatever they wanted.

When one athlete decided to skip practice in favor of something "more important," the coach realized things had gone too far and that the athletes were now controlling her. The athletes started showing a poor attitude in practice and an unwillingness to go all out in a game. The coach and I met and discussed ways she could be firmer with her athletes, yet fair. Our goal was to ensure that her athletes knew she was in charge and that she was there to serve them. During a meeting, she admitted to making mistakes and created new rules with the input of team members and her colleagues. She explained that the rules were aimed at keeping the team moving toward their goals and would be strictly enforced. Then the team and staff outlined fair consequences for those who broke the rules, such as writing letters of apology to the team or losing playing time.

Refuse to get caught in the trap of trying to please your athletes. Provide them with supportive, flexible guidance rather than catering to their every whim.

You don't serve anyone well when you allow athletes to tamper with your rules, regulations, and expected behavior. This coach's original approach led to complete chaos and lack of respect. Fortunately, this team turned things around immediately; the coach was determined to make it right and to stick to her word. She was willing to bench the starters and risk losing a game if that's what it took to show how serious she was about sticking to the rules. She was prepared for some of the athletes to test her at first to see just how serious she was, but she knew that in a short time they would get the message or have to deal with the consequences of not being a part of the team.

Being firm and fair also requires that you control your temper and model composure during difficult times. One popular trick that helps many people keep their cool is to wait 10 seconds before reacting in such situations. Count to 10 slowly while taking three deep breaths before speaking. This will relax you. If you do "lose it," an apology is an appropriate way to bounce back.

If controlling your anger is a particular challenge for you and you've gotten yourself into trouble because of it, seek professional help to learn other techniques to help control your anger. Attending to this obstacle will make you a more successful coach.

Accept and Affirm

Compliments and positive comments about athletes' efforts are important for the development of young athletes in their quest to be the best. Some coaches bark orders, while others are like machines with practice drills. Sometimes a quiet "good job" will go

Coach Jimmy Johnson applauds during practice. Praise helps athletes at all levels to persevere and to succeed.

far. Giving an athlete timely praise and attention reinforces all good efforts on the road to optimal performance.

There are a number of ways to creatively praise your athletes. I know of a hard-working high school soccer coach who, along with her staff, takes the time to make a short phone call to one or two parents of players after each game to praise the individual athlete's efforts and point out how the athlete can become even more effective on the field. She asks the parent to pass the words on to the athlete. Even players who experience little or no playing time get calls periodically that express the coaches' appreciation for their participation on the team. The fact that the team happens to be a perennial league power with each athlete willing to go the distance for the staff must have something to do with the positive attention they receive on and off the field.

Look for moments during practice when an athlete seems to be giving a full effort, stop play, and say, "Josh, I love when you do that; I love your intensity." You may not choose these exact words in your praise; discover what feels comfortable for you.

Contrast this approach with that of another coach in the same conference who routinely benches his players during a game if they make a mistake. Benching athletes for mistakes sends the clear message that if they commit an error, they won't get the opportunity to play. Who wouldn't play with less aggressiveness and more anxiety under such leadership? Athletes play tentatively if they focus on the penalty rather than the possibility of success. This coach rarely demonstrates positive feedback, choosing instead to focus on what the athletes fail to do rather than reinforcing and nurturing positive steps they may have made toward improvement.

Consistently negative criticism makes players feel inadequate, unworthy, not good enough. With lowered confidence, an athlete will refuse to take any risks, which will stymie not only his progress toward greatness, but also his passion for competition. Athletes in environments that emphasize weakness eventually give up. Those who are complimented and praised for their strengths tend to stick with it and achieve personal success. They are more likely to take chances during a competitive event—and therefore improve—than to hold back out of fear of being chastised for doing wrong.

*Demonstrate your confidence in an athlete's ability,
even if she has made some mistakes.*

All athletes, regardless of their level of play, need praise. All need acceptance and a sense of belonging in a team or program. We all blossom with a strong foundation of positive self-esteem. Coaches are more effective when they search for ways to satisfy the important psychological and emotional needs of those they coach through the experience of sport. Consider the following creative ways successful coaches can nurture their athletes.

• Be sure that all players have a defined role on the team, and compliment them when they embrace their roles. For example, an athlete may be called on to "work out" the team's backup goalie before a game, or may be expected to show great intensity coming off the bench, or perhaps may be counted on to assist rather than score. (In chapters 4 and 5 you will discover how to define players' roles within a team while still giving an athlete enough room to grow within that role.)

• Let players know that they count and that you appreciate their efforts. An occasional note, phone call, or e-mail can do wonders whether during the season or the off season. Even if you see a player at practice each day, communication away from the practice or game setting requires a special effort that an athlete appreciates. Commenting on good deeds at a practice or in a game is also important. Whenever it seems appropriate to take the time, don't hesitate. Just be sure that you are sincere in your praise.

• Look for ways to demonstrate your confidence in athletes' abilities. Avoid yanking them from the playing arena after they make a mistake. Instead, talk to them after the competition about how to correct such a mistake or prevent it from happening in the future. If an athlete demonstrates a lack of awareness of making a mistake and does so again and again, you may want to pull the athlete out and explain right there, one-on-one, what they need to focus on.

• Instill courage in your athletes; give them permission to make mistakes, knowing that they can learn from them.

• Present the opportunity for personal recognition rewards: player of the week (defense and offense), best efforts in practice or competitions, sportsmanship, communication, and so forth. Enable all players within their roles to have a chance to get personally recognized. All who perform their roles well should be recognized. Posting names in a visible place and having a monthly celebration pizza night, for example, to celebrate these players might be a helpful way to recognize such excellence.

Learn to Step Aside

Making the time to serve your athletes means frequently asking yourself, *How can I help this athlete or situation?* This doesn't necessarily mean that you have to fix every problem. Repair work may be called for on occasion, but many creative coaches find they serve best by stepping aside and getting out of the way to allow athletes to work out their own problems or to come to their own solutions. Too many of us micromanage situations. The best coaches, like the best waiters and the best teachers, are often those you hardly notice. They quietly do what is necessary when it is necessary and otherwise leave you alone.

Tex Winter, Phil Jackson's assistant coach with the Bulls and Lakers, says Phil is often able to step aside when necessary. On one occasion when chaos was breaking loose on the court, Winter screamed at Phil to take a timeout. Word has it that Phil shouted back to Tex to let it be, that they could work it out themselves. Phil was able to see the big picture and put emotions aside. And the players did solve the problem themselves.

You may remember the Bulls' 1994 NBA playoff game when Scottie Pippen, disagreeing with his coach's decision to use another player to take the last shot and to use Pippen as a decoy, refused to play. Such behavior sabotaged what the Bulls stood for, and Coach Jackson was furious. After the game, in the locker room, rather than step in and take over, Jackson said to the team something like "What was broken was sacred . . . it hurts us . . . now you have to work this out." He and his staff then left the room to let the team resolve the issue.

Be willing to give extra time to an athlete in need of development, either before or after practice. You can recruit the team captains and other team members to contribute their time to help teammates in this way, as well. Look for ways to provide optimal conditions for each athlete to succeed. For example, in sports where athletes can practice alone or with one another, have them create a time to practice that is more convenient to their schedule.

A successful coach creates an environment in which athletes can flourish. In addition to setting up one-on-one meetings with athletes, involve them in activities that promote team bonding and cohesion (discussed in greater detail in chapter 4). For example, many details need attention for the program to run smoothly, such as gathering equipment before and after practice, moving benches around, and setting up the practice area. Make a list of important tasks like these and have athletes sign up to take care of them on a weekly or monthly basis.

Enlist your captains to take on more leadership responsibilities by finding ways to better serve their teammates. Being a team captain is an honor and a responsibility; emphasize the ways captains can best serve the team. Think about the details you attend to as a coach that can be handled effectively by these leaders for the benefit of the entire team. For example, delegate responsibility for the collection and storage of team equipment. Or ask captains to be in charge of holding team meetings to collect feedback from the athletes about the program. Ask your captains if they are aware of what needs to be done and see if they are willing to take it on. Each program I have worked with has team captains serving the team in these ways, enhancing team leadership and enthusiasm.

The most important thing to keep in mind is to send the message that within the guidelines and boundaries established by your program, all in your program are there to serve one another on the road to realizing their greatest athletic and human potential. Good things happen when everyone stays in touch with this frame of mind and heart.

Serve and Be Served

In tennis, you serve a ball as an offer to begin the game with a readiness to receive the return of service. So it is with coaching: you instill in your athletes a sense of their own greatness, and in return you both benefit from a nurturing environment.

Alan Kirkup, women's soccer coach at the University of Arkansas, encourages his athletes to ask themselves *How can I best serve my team?* as opposed to *How can I get more playing time?* He uses one-on-one meetings during the season between a staff coach and each player to ask this question. The staff conducts such meetings every other week for 20 minutes each. They also use this time to discover ways that the staff can be of greater help to the athlete's progress. The coach may ask, "How can we help you to get even better?" The coaches then get together and discuss how they will help. Alan discovered during such a meeting that one of the team's forwards was nervous about making mistakes during games and therefore played very tight. He and his staff gave her permission to make mistakes, reminding her that they'd rather see her take the chances and fail than not risk at all. She began to relax and play to her potential.

When I work with a coach who aspires to serve, I notice that the athletes are more willing to follow in those footsteps. It's then easy for me to suggest to an athlete how an attitude of selflessness and giving makes sense in building a strong, well-bonded team. Before long, a healthy give-and-take culture develops, in which coaches and athletes thrive together. This is discussed further in chapter 4, but for now, remember that the backbone of team cohesiveness is a strong sense of service. Athletes also need to recognize that their behaviors are part of serving the team. They are not doing themselves or their team a service by not conditioning or by not practicing at 100-percent effort to work toward more consistent, higher-level performance in competition.

Service ignites passion in those you serve.

One of my favorite exercises to do with coaches and their teams encourages the athletes to serve one another by affirming one another's strengths, which fosters an environment ideal for individual growth and success. It's called the *circle of affirmation*. Begin by having your staff and team sit in a circle. Each member of the team takes about two minutes to tell the person to his left something that is complimentary, affirmative, and validating (of course, avoid superficial or patronizing comments). The speaker should indicate why he appreciates the listener as a teammate and a person. After once around, go back to the right and continue the process. Coaches can join in or hold their comments for the end, addressing each athlete individually. For large teams like football, you may want to break the team up into smaller groups of 10 or 15 people. I find that a good time to hold this circle of affirmation is halfway through a season or before a tournament or championship game; however, you may work this into the schedule anytime you feel the need to bring the team closer.

I have used this exercise with 12 national championship teams before their Final Four appearances. It works best when a team has had some time to get to know one another. You will be amazed at the responses and at the effect it has on the strength of the team. I have discovered through these experiences that the way teams express themselves in these sessions translates into the way they express themselves in competition: open, receptive, respectful, daring, bold, and fearless. Also, a sense of individual empowerment carries over to the playing field. Team members are more willing to go the distance for one another on the field. They may not win, but they will never give up in an all-out effort to be victorious.

The first time I tried this exercise was with Bob Hansen's UCSC tennis team in 1989. When the meeting was over, everyone was fired up and wanted to play at that moment. They held on to that feedback and flew to Kalamazoo College for their Final Four appearance, where they won their first of four national championships.

From a single seed comes a fragrant, beautiful flower—all because you took the time and effort to cultivate it throughout its growth process. Creative coaches know that it is no different with coaching. They affirm, inspire, compliment, praise, and stroke the greatness within their athletes in an environment of hope and trust. All who remember the late Red Holzman, coach of the NBA champion New York Knicks, know how he inspired and affirmed with a tender touch by treating players like the adults they were and by having them take responsibility for their performance and conditioning. Players appreciated the way he would affirm their efforts. Former Knick Phil Jackson said of his mentor's tender touch, "He had a knack for compromise and conciliation . . . never overloaded you with advice. He doled it out in small packets. . . . He had a featherweight punch that hit you like a knockout blow."

- I work to create an environment in which athletes feel a sense of acceptance and belonging.

- When I conduct circles of affirmation on a consistent basis, I build strong bonds and team unity.

- I am a caring, positive leader who takes the time to compliment and encourage my athletes regularly in order to develop positive self-esteem and higher levels of performance.

Care for all athletes ready to sprout. Encourage all shoots to reach the sky. Feed the hunger of the athletes' heart and soul.

4

Forging Cohesiveness

Championship teams have in common athletes who are willing to serve for the greater good of the team.

The ancient war strategist Sun-Tzu believed that that the key to triumph in battle is unity of purpose and heart. Spoken over two thousand years ago, this statement has tremendous relevance for today's athlete. In an age in which many athletes are self-absorbed, in which *me* is the word of choice, we can use such wisdom and practice this virtue of selflessness. The lead must come from the coach. By communicating this concept and serving your athletes, you can instill in your athletes this unity of heart.

Sports history is filled with examples of the dramatic power of cohesiveness in team athletics. Emblazoned in the memories of many Americans is the family-like cohesion demonstrated by the United States Olympic hockey team in 1980. The whole country felt this bond and wanted to be a part of the team, rallying behind it. Then there was the United States women's soccer team, 1999 World Cup champions—a group of athletes who agreed to accept roles because their hearts and souls were into the team's journey to victory.

As they celebrate, members of the 1999 U.S. women's soccer team demonstrate the cohesion that led them to the championship.

That same special bond can exist on an individual level, between player and coach. In some cases the relationship results because the player is very much an extension of the coach in terms of leadership and commitment to team goals. The point guard in basketball, the center in hockey, the quarterback in football, and other positions involving direct implementation of the team's attack are common roles for athletes with whom the coach is especially close.

In other instances, a coach and player establish a high sense of trust and appreciation because of the trials they have endured and conquered together. Whether it's losing seasons, injuries, family hardships, or any of a host of obstacles, the two are joined at the hip because they have prevailed and, through the strife, have acknowledged the other's importance.

Fitting both scenarios is the relationship shared by Michigan State coach Tom Izzo and Mateen Cleeves. As a uniquely gifted floor leader in both basketball skills and personality, Cleeves was a coach's dream in terms of conducting the game plan on the court and reinforcing team goals in the locker room. However, Cleeves' behavior outside the game was less than stellar and combined with recurring injuries through his college career to challenge his coach's faith that he would deliver. But Izzo stood loyal, and in the end, the two walked off the court together for the last time celebrating an NCAA championship. Unified, cohesive efforts create such possibilities.

Five months before the start of their season, head coach Gail Goestenkors of the Duke women's basketball team approached me with her team's primary goal: a journey to the Final Four. They had the talent and, like any championship-level team, needed to work together to make it happen.

Team cohesion is much more than synergy, cooperation, unity, and harmony among athletes. At the root of true cohesion is selflessness, a willingness to see that the team goal is greater than the goal of any one athlete. In Duke's case, they had to go beyond their traditional notion of *team*—five players on the court assuming their positions, with players on the sidelines ready to rotate in—and learn how to serve one another, to accept a lesser individual role if necessary to go to the next level as a team. Each athlete had to be willing to accept the coach's decisions about what was the best way for her to contribute to this journey. A breakdown in this attitude and focus would weaken the bond and threaten their championship destiny.

The previous year, the team had reached the regional final, only to get eliminated before the Final Four by the Arkansas Razorbacks. They later attributed their loss to not clearly being able to see themselves in the Final Four. They admitted that when they found themselves so close to going, they questioned whether they were ready, whether they "deserved" it, and whether they had what it took. This self-doubt showed up in the way they played in that second half—very tentatively. They became determined not to let that happen again.

From that learning experience of losing and finding out that they hadn't really believed in themselves, they understood the importance of pulling together as a cohesive team, working closely together for the purpose of being in the Final Four, and believing that they deserved to be there. This learning—coupled with defining their team roles, performing daily meditations to remind them of their unified purpose (see page 84), and creating opportunities to strengthen their team bond—placed these warriors in position to realize their dream.

Define Team Roles

To get the Duke Blue Devils started in achieving their goal, each athlete was first asked to play her individual role for the team, regardless of the minutes she played. These roles, in some cases, were obvious to the coaches and players; in other cases, the coaches needed to help the players define their roles more clearly. Some were shooters, others rebounders, and still others were to come off the bench to play tenacious defense. Some didn't get to play much in games, but would be vital contributors in tough practice sessions or be ready to play immediately for an injured player.

In *Values of the Game*, Bill Bradley writes that "championships are not won unless a team has forged a high degree of unity, attainable only through the selflessness of each of its players," and that "untrammeled individualism destroys the chance for achieving victory" (page 43). Bradley's buddy and ex-teammate Phil Jackson agrees. In *Sacred Hoops*, Jackson notes that the real reason the Chicago Bulls won so often during his coaching years there was their power of oneness—the *we, not me* approach. The vision of the group imperative took precedence over individual glory. They were willing to serve one another, to accept and adapt to their roles for the good of the team.

A common quality I notice when working with championship-level teams is the athletes' unrelenting willingness to serve one another for the greater good of the team. This is true of the coaching staff, managers, trainers, and anyone else associated with the team. They ask, *How can I give more?* rather than *How can I get more?* This service translates to well-defined individual roles.

Synergy, cooperation, and cohesiveness are essential to team success in all sports, creating order, enthusiasm, focus, excitement, and deep levels of commitment. But athletes don't just "find" their own roles on a team—the roles are specified, at least to some extent, by their coach, who identifies and then communicates to an athlete, "We need you to do this," or "We need you in this way," or "Your role is essential to the team's progress." It's crucial to help athletes see the ways they contribute to the development and improvement of the team in training, practice, and competitions.

One of the best ways to discuss this with high school and collegiate team members is to have athletes write down their answers to the following questions:

How can I best serve my team in practices and training?

How can I best serve my team in competition?

Coaches can then sit down and discuss the athlete's answers with respect to the team goal. Coaches should act as guides and adjust a role if it's off-target. Coaches can suggest additional ways that an athlete can serve the team. If athletes define their roles and they are aligned with the program, they will have a greater investment in taking on that role.

It's up to the coach to say to an athlete, "You are the best at being a good practice player and can help the team the most in this role." If the athlete wants to fill another role, and that desire is realistic, tell him exactly what it will take to do so and guide him toward doing it.

Some athletes will need more help in defining this role than others. Be sure to go beyond simply defining an athlete's best role on a team; emphasize its importance to the overall mission of the team. Avoid pigeonholing athletes into just one possible role and encourage them to think more expansively and to take more risks. Those who rarely play in games need to see their contribution to team morale and spirit. Ask the athletes to give their all in practice and in the game by challenging one another to play at higher levels. Invite them to lead with great enthusiasm and fire. Selflessness is best experienced in the pursuit of victory in an environment of cooperation, friendship, support, mutual respect, and compassion.

Some athletes may not feel good about their chosen roles. Some who don't get the playing time, or don't get to participate in the event they want in a competition, may even threaten to walk away. Listen to an athlete's complaints and consider making a deal with him, such as, if he shows you he can do x and y, he will be given an opportunity. Try to provide the athlete an opportunity to prove to you they can play their desired role. For example, allow him to race or time trial in that particular distance that he wants to race, but doesn't usually have the chance to. An athlete's reaction to such an opportunity will give you a clue as to that athlete's level of commitment.

Have individual meetings with athletes who struggle with their role on their team. Athletes who are off track may display boredom, disgust, depression, anger, irritability, and other emotions related to not feeling needed. In such cases, have a talk with the athlete to see how you can work together to correct the problem. Some athletes' perceptions about how to serve may be at variance with the team's journey. For example, an athlete may perceive his service as an offensive contributor, yet the team needs him to give more on defense. Reply with something like, "We know you can score, and you'll get that opportunity; however, we really feel you can best serve the team with your relentless defensive play."

You can let others know how the team needs individual athletes in the specific roles they play as well; praise them at a press conference or to the fans, who may not realize that their contribution is important. Missouri basketball coach Quin Snyder, during his weekly radio broadcast, always finds ways to compliment and praise those athletes who usually get overlooked in the interviews. It's up to the coaching staff to find significant roles for everyone on the team and ways to communicate the importance of those roles, not only to the athlete, but to others interested in the team.

When athletes' roles are defined (and they are not written in stone—they can change when appropriate) write them on a master sheet and pass them out to all team members and staff. When the athletes see that their teammates are serving in various ways, this strengthens the team bond, creating a more cohesive unit.

Unconditional Service

Serving the team is what high-profile athletes like Kareem Abdul-Jabbar, Michael Jordan, Wayne Gretzky, Walter Payton, and numerous others were all about. Some lower-profile team players are also good examples of unconditional service. Dale Davis of the Indiana Pacers was voted to the NBA All-Star team not because of his scoring prowess, but because the league recognized that he served with the less glamorous skills that help a team win—great defense and rebounding. Dennis Rodman is another example of an athlete who has made a living by finding his service niche—rebounding. Great athletes are willing to sacrifice personal gain for the team. You see this in the sport of road cycling all the time. Lance Armstrong's Tour de France victories have

Tour de France winner Lance Armstrong and the U.S. Postal Service team members who supported him enjoy the victory parade.

only been possible because of his team members, the domestiques on his U.S. Postal Service team who bridge gaps, protect a key rider, or block other riders to secure a top spot for their rider.

Michael Jordan could have been the greatest scorer in NBA history, but if he had sought that goal, the Bulls probably would not have won all those championships. He was instead unselfish and put his teammates above his own glory. He often took extra time to help teach his teammates aspects of the game that made them better players. Scottie Pippen has credited Michael with helping him to elevate his game. Because these athletes weren't concerned about who got all the credit, their teams were much better than they would have been if selfishness had prevailed.

These athletes weren't always like this. It takes an astute coach to instill these qualities of service in an athlete. It was Phil Jackson who taught Jordan the value of becoming an unselfish player. Michael learned how to raise the level of play of his teammates by serving up the ball, making the Bulls more of a team threat. Serving the team in this way offers greater benefits than what an individual player can do alone. When Phil Jackson went to the Lakers, he taught the same lesson to Shaquille O'Neal. Take time to discuss with your team how these great athletes became even greater by serving their teams through unselfish play.

Before the arrival of Phil Jackson, the talented Bulls were struggling. One of Jackson's first moves was to introduce the team to Tex Winter's triangle motion offense, which requires all athletes to put individual needs aside. In this offense, every player on the floor gets to touch the ball instead of only the best shooters. If the rotation and motion creates an opening, that player takes it then and there, even if he has the poorest shooting percentage of the players on the floor. The offense forces athletes to give themselves totally to the group effort. Thinking and moving in unison empowered everybody on the team as they all became intricately involved in the offense and interconnected as athletes. What makes such a cohesive system fun is the exhilaration of losing oneself in the joy of playing automatically. The Bulls demonstrated a strong group intelligence—five players, one heart, one mind—and loved playing with one another for the good of the team.

Striving for Team Intelligence

Creative coaches, like Jackson, recognize the diverse talents and capabilities of the athletes in the group and find ways to harness them into a unit to foster team intelligence. You can do this by clarifying your athletes' roles and having them verbally commit to performing them together. The sooner this is done, the better. Communication between players and staff during preseason is crucial in the unifying process. As the team grows together, appropriate changes can keep the team unified.

Championship teams know that each athlete needs to surrender self-interest for the greater good of the team if the team is to win. Paradoxically, in this way the team contributes to each athlete's individual good. The Chinese share a perspective on the difference between heaven and hell: Each is an enormous banquet with delectable dishes on huge round tables. All at the banquets are given chopsticks five feet long. In the banquet in hell, people struggle to manipulate these awkward utensils, give up out of frustration, and starve. In heaven, everyone serves the person across the table and each becomes abundantly full. Create opportunities for the athletes to serve one another. In tennis, an accomplished starter could hit with a new, less talented teammate to help the athlete improve. Or a nonstarter on a lacrosse team could fire shots into the cage to help the goalkeeper get more experience.

Canadian geese provide an excellent example of effective teamwork. By flying together in a V formation, the flock can travel 71 percent farther than one goose could fly in the same amount of time. The geese honk encouragement to one another, helping those who are discouraged to keep up the pace. If a bird is sick or wounded, it flies out of formation, accompanied by friends who stay with it until it recovers.

Realistically, you might find that not all athletes buy into this notion; they've been too indoctrinated by the selfish messages that permeate modern culture. With these athletes, creating unity and a spirit of cohesiveness can be an uphill battle. I know of a high school star who was convinced, thanks to those close to him, that he could be playing in the NBA by his sophomore year in college. Believing this, he was forever forcing shots that weren't there, trying to demonstrate his prowess with stats and flair. Finally, his coach had to sit him down and define his role, and pointed out how he could become a better athlete by working within the team. When this player took the coach's suggestions and fulfilled his best role, he began to get more open shots and help his team to victories. Had this player not accepted his role, he would have struggled for much of the season and perhaps might have been a benchwarmer or left the team. Many athletes, having been raised in a culture that emphasizes *me* rather than *we,* find it difficult to accept selfless action and a more interdependent role with their teammates. But when they do, magic seems to take place.

Creative coaches know that they can build a team from a nucleus of those who desire to create a family, allowing others to join when they're ready. You can't legislate selfless team values; simply model what you can and let the rest join when they see what they are missing. This works in most cases. When it doesn't, expose the athlete to the alternatives within the system and have the player decide what she wishes to do, given the choices. A player may even opt for leaving the team, which may benefit all involved. If a player is unwilling to fit into your team's program, be up-front with her. There is no need to get upset or personal. Simply state it as it is and let the athlete know the team needs to move forward.

Meditate on Your Team's Purpose

To help the Duke women's basketball team develop their cohesiveness and ensure they were all on the same page as a team, we created a ritual that they could use daily. This exercise can help any team. The players and coaches come together before each practice and game to meditate, visualize, and affirm their strengths, bonds, and purpose for 10 minutes. Meditation cleared their minds and allowed them to visualize their practice or game plan and affirm, "Regardless of outcomes, we play like fearless, courageous champions. We deserve to be a Final Four team and a national champion team." This time together was sacred for the Blue Devils, a time to create a strong bond. It was a quiet time to focus on the team as a unit, a team with a destiny.

As each game of the season was played, one could sense the cohesion getting stronger. Much credit for this was due to these regular meditation exercises that helped them refocus and regroup daily on their mission and goals; they began to play together as one, a well-oiled machine with each part working in sync with the others. They were fun to watch and had fun in this process. They won their conference with a 15-1 record and marched into the NCAA tournament, just one year after the upsetting Arkansas game.

They were again in a regional final facing the number-one seed, the University of Tennessee; the Lady Vols were practically shoo-ins to win the championship. Duke came out fired up; the team synergy and cohesiveness were electrifying, and the crowd went berserk. Love for the game and one another emanated from these women. Their unified efforts stunned Tennessee as the Devils realized their vision of a berth in the Final Four. Their cohesion was demonstrated by their constant communication on and off the court, their strong verbal support for one another, their willingness to gather around an injured player and show encouragement, and the obvious closeness between coaches and athletes. They had demonstrated this cohesion throughout the season, and by the time they found themselves in this position again they were able to use it to their greatest advantage.

Create Opportunities to Unite

Creating team unity and cohesiveness takes time. For this reason, coaches need to address the issue from the first day of practice and be attentive to it throughout the season. Some teams will be more naturally cohesive than others due to a certain team chemistry that unites the athletes. While a coach can recruit athletes who display personal characteristics that are congruent with the program, more often team chemistry simply happens and can't be predicted. Rest assured, even if your team doesn't seem to have "natural" team chemistry, the following strategies can help develop cohesion in just about any group of athletes.

Coaches play a crucial role in helping their teams develop unity. Demonstrating unity among assistants and supporting staff is a good start. If you model togetherness and a unity of heart, your athletes will be more receptive to learning and more open to ways to unite as a team. Many of the coaches I work with conduct team meetings to discuss the concept of team unity and to ask the athletes how to strengthen the bond. Here are some ideas that these teams and coaches have used with success.

Self-Define

Make a time for the team and staff to come together in a group and answer the question *Who are we?* One team may answer, "We are the NCAA national champions. We are bold, aggressive, courageous, fearless, audacious, tenacious, national-class athletes." Another team may answer, "We are the class act of the Big Ten" or "We are the standard by which excellence is measured." Discuss how and why you are what these words describe. Such self-defining indicates pride and self-respect and brings team members together under one banner.

Follow up this activity by expressing these self-definitions on paper and posting them in the locker room. These "spirit slogans" can keep you united with a common theme. The words affirm that you are more alike than different. They are touchstones that, when spoken, help athletes to remember that they are family, clan, tribe, united as a whole.

Create a Chant or Cheer

A team cheer or chant can affirm that coming together, win or lose, helps your athletes play together. Think of words that indicate who you are and recite them out loud together before practice or contests. Make it personal, short, and emotional if you can. These words become a touchstone helping you to focus on your strength as a unit. Use the words you created in your self-definition. Get the entire team involved in the project. Have the team say the chant before a special practice, before or during each game, or after every team meeting.

Share Words That Inspire

Have a player read an inspirational poem, or have each player pass out an inspirational quote or saying before each game or at the start of each practice week. I know an athlete who writes a poem before each game with words that relate personally to her team and their mission. She reads it before the team runs out on the field. The coaches encourage her poetic talent to create these moments of bonding.

One cross country team modified this activity by having a team member collect a song from each member of the team (it could be something that reminded that person of their team or running, or anything). Each person (even the coaches and support staff) submitted a tape of her chosen song, and the songs were then compiled onto one tape and duplicated for each team member. Another team member designed a cover for the compilation tape using a team photo. Everyone got a kick out of the songs each person on the team had chosen, especially the coach's pick—a Metallica song! It helped each team member to learn more about her teammates and coach. It became the team's favorite tape to listen to in the van on the way to meets.

Plan Get-Togethers
Team members do not have to be best friends to have cohesion. However, it does help to get together occasionally to socialize and "play" together outside of practice or games. Team parties, picnics, outings, and dinners (especially if everyone pitches in to cook or brings something) are excellent ways to encourage togetherness. These are opportunities to get to understand and accept different personalities, which is essential to team synergy. Coaches need to encourage this, but let the athletes handle the details.

Create Nicknames
Lighthearted, positive nicknames can spur on spirit and unity, giving team members a sense of specialness and belonging. Make sure everyone is comfortable with the name. In many instances, this happens naturally within teams. A creative coach could ask a team to place their names on their locker doors, using a name that they care to be known as. It's fun to find out these names and use them when addressing the athlete.

Plan a Retreat
When appropriate, create a time for renewal, a spiritual team retreat in the off-season. Take the time to laugh, play, and notice

why you feel good about one another. Choose a place that provides rope courses and other devices for active ways to build the team and strengthen the bond.

Visualize Unity

Try this visualization exercise with your team sitting in a circle. Give your athletes the following instructions: Mentally scan the room, looking at your teammates dressed in uniform. Imagine them milling around, stopping to talk to one another. They are shaking hands, smiling, and hugging one another. Go over to each member and express your appreciation for his contribution to the team and say how fortunate you feel being a part of this group. When everyone has done this, you are now ready, as a team, to go about your performance. See yourself and the team playing against the opponent. Notice how "together" you are, how each is contributing to others' great performance. Your team is unstoppable and as fluid as a well-oiled machine. See your team's performance being the model of team harmony and execution. Feel the exhilaration as you all play together to secure victory.

Visualize together the ideal you wish for team unity.

Try one or any combination of these ideas to develop your team's cohesion. In addition, consider how clearly defined individual roles help all athletes understand how they best contribute to the total team effort and contribute to bonding and cohesion. It's easier to feel part of a group when you truly know your function, your role, and how you serve your team.

Red Auerbach, former coach of the NBA champion Boston Celtics, said that you don't necessarily win with the best five players; rather, you win with the best team, the five who fit together best. Once a player becomes bigger than the team, you no longer have a team. Team cohesion requires a coach to be constantly aware of team dynamics and willing to create changes in roles when it could benefit the chemistry of the players. To help ensure such chemistry and team cohesion, recruit players who fit your profile of a team player. It's not always good to select athletes only on their physical abilities, especially if they have an attitude problem. Choosing your team may not be easy, but it helps if you can get the right physical and emotional balance with your players.

There is no one way to guarantee a cohesive team. You can't always make the right choice, but following the guidelines outlined in this chapter will help you get on track. Can your team win without cohesion? Quite possibly it can—but *with* cohesion, it can probably play at a higher level than it will without it.

- To create an environment of selflessness, I identify the essential function of each athlete on the team.

- I creatively facilitate team unity.

- When I create cohesion, I put my team in position to fulfill their potential.

Now that you have instilled the attributes of cohesion and service in your team, your athletes are better prepared for you to step aside a bit. Let go of some control and guide them to their questions rather than forcing them to go there. They'll be better prepared to be proactive in their destiny.

part II

Leading With a Purpose

5

Providing Guidance

Be clear about your mission, and you will naturally make the right decisions to achieve it.

Have you heard the saying that if a rancher truly wants to have greater control over his cows, he should move the fences back to give them more room? The same is true in coaching—when you try to control or micromanage players or situations, athletes tighten up and rebel. On the other hand, if you assume a completely hands-off approach, things can fall apart—you do still need a fence, after all!

One of the hallmarks of successful, creative coaches is that they guide their athletes by establishing well-defined boundaries with enough room for the athletes to expand and grow. They refuse to coddle their athletes, yet create a supportive environment that helps them to realize their potential. They understand that serving their athletes means nurturing them, yet being firm enough to help them learn to make decisions on their own by providing an environment that allows them to do so. These coaches don't exert complete control; they include the athletes in setting team guidelines, rules, and other policies. I have learned from these masters that when athletes are not overwhelmed by a strict, authoritative coach, a team unified toward achieving their mission emerges. By guiding athletes rather than trying to control their every move, a coach encourages them to be more self-reliant or self-coached.

Appropriate guidance creates an atmosphere that encourages others to think and accomplish for themselves. When this happens, athletes work together in support of team goals, producing the best outcomes and fostering a sense of accomplishment. This type of coaching style is a *do with* rather than a *do to* approach, in which a coach works *with* athletes and gives them more and more responsibility to shape their own roles within the team. You might give the athletes some freedom to decide on certain drills and to create activities for a segment of practice; you can ease this process by offering them a few options to pick from. Or perhaps they can have a say in what training will be done during the off-season.

There are times when this style of coaching is inappropriate or can backfire. For example, very young or immature athletes may not respond well to a *do with* approach. Working with such players often requires you to be more direct, using a *do to* approach that tells the athletes specifically what they need to do.

You may try to let the athletes guide themselves and see how they respond—you can always adjust your guidance depending on what you find. Proceed with caution to get a feel for how much leeway you can give. Creative coaching requires that you be flexible in your style; use a more hands-off guidance approach when your athletes are responsible, mature players and a more directive approach with those who need it. Athletes who are guided and who play a role in decision-making will see that when they take on responsibility, they are rewarded with greater freedom to choose and control their lives.

Several coaches I've worked with tell me that their attempts to micromanage and control their athletes have created mistrust, lack of cooperation, and a loss of faith in their program or coaching system. Athletes react to too many controls, prohibitions, and harsh interventions by resisting with counterforce and resentment; they outwardly do what the coaches tell them to do, but inwardly turn off. Many successful coaches argue that athletes who are micromanaged tend to show less excitement, enthusiasm, spirit, and willingness to go the extra mile when needed.

Establish Clear Boundaries

To guide athletes effectively, it is crucial to establish clear, direct boundaries that give them room to roam within a defined structure. You may consider involving the players in setting up these boundaries, thus giving them more of an investment in keeping to these guidelines. The following strategies will help you to guide more effectively within the team boundaries.

Set the Ground Rules

When you contemplate how to formulate your team policies and rules, keep in mind that *less is more*. Do you want to spend your valuable time policing your athletes, or do you want to watch them operate and grow within legitimate, manageable guidelines? Having fewer rules—but making the ones you do have meaningful— can give you more power because you have fewer details to enforce and because you teach athletes to use their freedom responsibly.

Paul Wardlaw, head coach of the University of Iowa women's tennis team, has one rule: *Do the right thing.* This clear directive covers a myriad of situations and makes the global assumption that his athletes are reasonable, mature, and wise enough to know right from wrong in most situations. If one of his athletes does not do the right thing, he lets the team determine how that athlete is handled. They discuss in detail what "the right thing" is in the particular situation and ask that athlete to cooperate with doing what's right from now on. This rule is particularly effective for enforcing curfew and standards for attendance and punctuality, sportsmanship, and effort in class and on the court. Paul simply asks, "Lisa, was coming to practice late the right thing to do?" The athlete usually gets the point and explains why it happened. If the excuse is unacceptable (and most are), he and the team may decide on a fitting consequence, such as coming early the next practice or staying late to make up the missed time.

Fortunately for Paul, he's recruited a very mature group. Other coaches may have athletes who need more boundaries and structure. Moreover, most athletes like the structure of having a number of rules and looking for ways to function at higher levels within the boundaries of the system. Rules make your athletes accountable for their behavior. They create order and provide the blueprints for building a well-disciplined organization.

Less is more.
Too many rules can be a burden to enforce.

The idea is to establish a balance between too many and too few rules by creating a few good rules that encompass many situations. One way to do this is to go back to your team's goals and discuss with the team what rules they need to outline to achieve this mission. Start by writing out your team's mission and then build rules toward achieving this mission, giving attention to the following primary targets for establishing clear, concise rules.

• **Curfew.** A reasonable curfew can be reached by consensus of team and staff. Take into account what your athletes need to fit into their daily schedules, including the rest they need to function optimally and stay healthy. Provide guidelines for curfew when the team travels, as well. High school coaches can set a curfew and discuss it with parents to help them enforce it.

• **Tardiness and absenteeism.** It is important to have strict guidelines for these two areas, especially for repeat offenders. Consider a zero tolerance policy for being late or absent for practices, games, and other team events. Set an exact time and teach athletes that they are responsible for being there at that time, not one minute late—no excuses.

• **Equipment care.** All athletes, regardless of age or grade, need to take turns making sure team equipment is available and cleaned up after use. I suggest having sign-up sheets and rotating the athletes through these chores. By making such duties part of the team policy, you can build them into the team's practice routine.

• **Alcohol, tobacco, and other drugs.** Use of these substances is contrary to your mission. Make it clear what your policy is and what the consequences for violating it are. Again, I recommend simply establishing a clear-cut zero tolerance policy.

• **Disrespect toward staff and team.** Name-calling, swearing, putdowns, hitting, and other forms of abuse should not be tolerated.

Talk about this with your team up-front. Note that such disrespect is the beginning of the deterioration of the team bond. Cohesion is not possible with such abuse. Also, establish a policy that any team member resorting to such disrespect will be required to write a letter of apology that states positive words to counteract the negative abuse.

• **Attendance of team functions.** Address what the consequences are for refusal to attend mandatory functions such as talks, meetings, gatherings, presentations, award ceremonies, and so on.

• **Classroom issues.** Rules regarding a certain grade point average for the team could be established (raising the bar of that set by the district, department, or other governing bodies). Attendance and doing (or at least attempting to do) homework should be expected of any student-athlete. For coaches of nonscholastic teams, the responsibilities for setting rules regarding academics should fall on parents. The coach can work with parents for setting up such rules, but the parents must enforce them.

These parameters are suggestions only; you can tailor them to your coaching style and team or athlete objectives. The bottom line is to keep your list of rules simple. Remember that rules are the necessary backup plans in case your regular routine and procedures are violated. It's better to give more attention to the procedures than to emphasize what will happen when all goes wrong. If your routines and procedures are stimulating and motivating, there probably will be little need for many rules. Still, it's helpful to establish the boundaries your team can operate best under and establish the consequences for going outside the boundaries.

*Focus on the routines and procedures
of your team rather than the consequences
of not adhering to them.*

As you put together your basic rules list, consider the following guidelines to help you fine-tune each of your team rules. I call these the *8 Cs of cooperation.*

8 Cs of Cooperation

Cocreate. Have your team work together with you to establish reasonable rules. When they have a say in them, they will have a greater investment in carrying them out. In this way, you don't become the "heavy" all of the time, policing the athletes around the clock. Athletes will tend to keep one another honest. Regardless, you are there to make sure consequences are enforced.

Clarity. Players need to understand the entire meaning of each rule. Clearly state the intention and function of each one. Part of this clarity is to discuss the consequences for not adhering to the rules. Here's an example: Anyone possessing drugs, alcohol, or illegal substances at any time while associated with the program will be dismissed from the team. The rule and consequence are very clear. On the other hand, a rule such as "Do not disrespect staff" is open to interpretation. Just what constitutes disrespect? Better to state the rules as "No swearing, name-calling, or put-downs."

Concise. Make rules short and to the point. Less is more, and simple is strong. "Lights out at 10" is concise. "Make sure you get plenty of rest; don't get less than seven hours of sleep each night before practice days and not less than eight before competition days" is not concise.

Copy. Write all rules on a poster and hang it in the locker room. Have all athletes sign their names to the board. State these positively—what to do, rather than what not to do. You can even get the athletes involved by making this a team activity. Provide athletes with a copy of these as well to take home with them.

Consistent. Assure that the rules are fair and that you are consistent in your enforcement. Stars and starters should not get preferential treatment. This takes us back to the concept of fairness, an important part of consistency in setting and enforcing rules.

Change. When an athlete or team outgrows the rules, be flexible enough to consider changing or adapting them. Do not change a rule while it's being violated; negotiate this later. For example, you may need to adjust your curfew during finals week to give extra hours in the evening to study. Keep in mind your team's mission when adjusting. For example, you may have a regular curfew at 10, but you decide to change it to 11 for one week only, knowing that your athletes will still get plenty of rest.

Consequences. Every athlete should know the consequences of breaking a rule. The first time a rule is broken, the consequences should be less than for repeat offenses (unless you have established a zero tolerance policy for the offense). Be sure athletes understand what happens to those who break rules. You might even get your athletes to play a role in coming up with these consequences as well. Athletes are often more harsh with themselves than you would be. You may need to temper their ideas and have the final say. The important thing is to work toward a consensus as to what is fair. Work to match the consequence with the offense—for example, if an athlete gets to practice late, he must come at least 30 minutes early next time.

Compliment. Reinforce athletes for following the rules. A simple, sincere statement like "good job" or "nice work" will suffice.

Model the Behavior You Expect

Naturally, it's important that you are bound by the same guidelines as your athletes where appropriate, and that you demonstrate correct behavior at all times. For example, coming to practice on time and doing what you expect of your athletes is important if you wish to gain the respect of your team.

History tells us that in ancient times, the most respected generals didn't set up canopies in the heat or wear leather in the cold for their own comfort; rather, they experienced the same conditions as their soldiers, the same toil, hunger, and thirst. They modeled what they valued and expected from those they led. In return, their soldiers admired them and were willing to go to battle for them.

So it is with coaches; realize that by modeling good things for those you lead, you create more respect and cooperation for your program. Think about the message you would send to your players if you were to yell at a referee, use foul language, be intoxicated in public, or in any other way fall short of the standards you demand from your athletes. What do you wish to teach others through sport? Creative coaches make the effort to narrow the gap between how they behave and what they expect from those they lead. The most powerful tool in your coaching bag is your own example—walk your talk. Others will listen more intently and learn more quickly if you pave the way. Notice what happens when you demonstrate the dedication and devotion to your mission that you ask of the athletes.

Model what you wish to teach. Walk your talk.

Have you ever considered looking for ways to participate in the drills, exercises, and fitness regimes that you give to your athletes? How do you think your athletes would respond to your lifting weights, stretching, or running with them? Several coaches I work with partake in fitness programs with athletes and have had strong positive reactions from them. Harry Groves, head track and field coach at Penn State, often runs or bikes beside his athletes when they train so that he may observe them more closely and encourage them. Quin Snyder can usually be found in the weight room along with his staff a few times each week. His athletes eat this up. This kind of participation can make a coach's credibility blossom. If you want to have a positive influence on your athletes, ask of yourself what you ask of them. A ripple effect occurs; your influence begins with you and flows outward.

This ripple effect is also evident when it comes to good sportsmanship. Pat Summitt, coach of the six-time national champion University of Tennessee women's basketball team, believes that this responsibility also falls on the coach. "I'm not going into a press conference and criticize an opponent," says Pat. Robert Frederich, athletics director of the University of Kansas, agrees with Coach Summitt. He claims that when the head coach sets the tone, the coach can make a difference in academics, sportsmanship, and many other areas of their athletes' lives.

Coach Pat Summit models the good sportsmanship she expects of her athletes.

Of course, many coaches have failed to model what they wish to teach. Not long ago, 40 nationally recognized distance runners gathered at an elite training camp to learn from some of the more prominent coaches in the United States. One member of the coaching staff offered a probing and comprehensive clinic on proper diet and nutrition for these aspiring athletes. This well-intentioned professional happened to be quite overweight and out of shape. The athletes' evident low attention spans and joking comments were clues that they had difficulty taking his talk to heart. One athlete remarked to another, "Yeah, follow his plan, and we'll look like him."

There are many ways that you can serve as a model for your athletes. First, consider how you outwardly express yourself in the following situations:

- How do you cope with failure?
- What are ways that you bring out the best in others?
- How do you demonstrate desire, a willingness to do what it takes to get a job done?
- How do you handle pressure and adversity on and off the court?
- How do you exhibit patience and persistence on the road to excellence?
- How do you create balance in your life each day?
- How do you give respect to others?
- Are you prepared?
- How do you deal with criticism?
- How do you listen?
- How do you make good decisions?
- How do you show that you care?
- How do you celebrate?
- How do you set realistic developmental goals?
- How do you give to others?
- How do you accept responsibility for your actions?

Let these questions guide you and your staff in your work and serve as reminders of those qualities you want to model for your athletes. Consider having the coaching staff address one question each week and discuss how to best do what the question asks. Search for ways that would help you to do the things you don't do now.

Make Informed, Firm Decisions

You've probably noticed how much easier it is to make decisions when you are clear about your program's goals or mission. With a clear purpose in mind, the next essential ingredient in making firm, sound decisions is *information;* the more you have, the easier it is.

Taking the time to learn as much as you can about new recruits and prospective team members, including their training needs and goals, will help you create a true marriage between athletes and your program philosophy. Go out of your way to gather information from athletes' former coaches, friends, and teammates. Let recruits spend time with your team so that all involved can get a sense about the compatibility of this player with your team and program.

The learning doesn't stop with just the newer members of your team, though. Learn as much as possible about your athletes and staff. Knowing the backgrounds and lives of those who are already on board helps you make solid decisions when confronting personal and behavioral problems. By being prepared with this information, you are better able to guide your team with wise decisions.

Sometimes, to make the best decision you need to wait for more data, information, and input from others. A good strategy to use when waiting for additional information and being asked to give an answer in the meantime is to be direct and honest: "I'm not sure at this moment, and I'd like more time to contemplate what's happening." Then research the situation and consult with your experts on the matter.

It's often wiser to put off making a decision than to make a decision that feels wrong and backfires. For example, when athletes get into trouble with the law, coaches are often pressured to make immediate decisions on the athlete's status with the team. In such cases it's prudent for the coach to wait on making a decision until the school or the court gathers all of the facts about what happened. Such a situation arose recently when a high school football player was accused of rape after Michigan State University had offered him a scholarship. At the time, MSU's position was that if the player was found guilty, the scholarship offer would be revoked. If the player was found not guilty, they would honor the offer.

If you feel the pressure to make a decision without having a clear vision and enough information, you can always *provisionally* decide. Several creative coaches I've worked with have success-fully adopted temporary plans with the stipulation that they could reevaluate at any time. They don't come across as wishy-washy, because they make it clear at the outset that this is a *provisional* decision. For example, you might say, "Let's go with this for now [giving your reason for doing so] and revisit the decision after we have more information." This takes away the pressure of having to make the right decision without enough data. This type of deci-sion-making process is used often by heads of business organiza-tions in order to keep things moving and productive without be-ing unfair. It requires you to trust your best intuitive judgment, the result of your experience.

Putting off making a decision until you have all the facts is often the right decision to make.

Keep in mind, however, that a coach who uses such a tactic on a regular basis may be viewed as someone whose decisions don't stick. Therefore, use this approach only when you feel fairly cer-tain that it's the right decision and forward movement is impor-tant. Never do this, however, if you can't live with the possibility of the decision being wrong.

The easier route is to establish hard-and-fast guidelines and rules on which you will base all decisions. But that makes about as much sense as a goalie failing to consider the respective strength and weaknesses, tendencies, and situational factors ev-ery time a different opposing player attacks the net. While the fundamentals might remain the same, each response needs to be tailored to best address the particular circumstance.

Legendary high school basketball coach, Morgan Wootten, ad-mitted to wanting everything cut-and-dried early in his career. He soon learned that such an approach was too simplistic. Perhaps this is most evident with regard to setting penalties for disciplin-ary problems. Wootten recounted that he automatically kicked off two star players from his DeMatha High team for missing cur-few by 15 minutes. After talking with each player individually, he learned that they had legitimate excuses and regretted the hasty decision that could well have hurt the players' chances with some colleges that were recruiting them. This put him in the awkward position of having to renounce his earlier decision to dismiss the players.

The lesson is: don't paint yourself into a corner. Establish a sound philosophy and a core set of guidelines for on and off the court that all can agree to. Then, as the season evolves and specific circumstances arise, *think* through each matter (albeit quickly, at times), to see if the decision you are inclined to make is, in fact, best. Creative problem solving can only be engaged in if the mind is more open than closed. That may sound wishy-washy to some, but it's also smart—and more effective.

A decisive coach will also create opportunities for his assistants, administrators, and athletes to contribute to the decision-making process. Collect data from all involved in a program and compare it to your best intuitive judgment, then take what makes sense. The final decision and responsibility are all yours. Thank others for their time and efforts and remind them that after considering their input, you will come to a resolution and make a decision.

Learn how much more effective you can be when you encourage others to participate in the decision-making process. Cindy Timchal's athletes love it when she gives them the objectives of the practice and asks for their input on how to achieve these goals. She provides this information just before practice once a week or every two weeks throughout the season. When they decide what drills to use, they naturally have a greater investment in performing them to the best of their ability. By letting the athletes decide, you have made a more effective, influential decision that affects more than just a practice session.

Encourage athletes to participate in the decision-making process, particularly as it pertains to them.

Allow for Adaptability

Every coach should have a master plan—a logistical presentation of their vision for the next year or season. Typically, such plans contain the monthly, weekly, and daily building blocks necessary to achieving the goals to which the team has committed. These more specific plans include points of emphasis and targets for particular times of the season. Even more detailed are the practice plans designating exactly what is to be covered and when for each session.

Such advance planning is essential, but if that was all it took to coach, computer-based organizers would be much more effective than humans. In the real world, plans take us only so far before we are required to adjust because of unforeseen circumstances.

Truly creative coaches are able to assimilate the new conditions into their original plan, determine how this will impact their master plan and primary objectives, and adjust their more specific monthly, weekly, and daily practice plans accordingly. A season-ending injury to a star athlete, an unexpected slump in the heart of the schedule, disciplinary or grade problems involving multiple players, and so on can derail an inflexible sports program.

That's why adaptability is essential in coaching. Leaving a little leeway in less certain aspects of the program allows you to respond more quickly and more effectively than if you had eliminated alternative approaches. So don't feel guilty about keeping your options open. Sometimes the decision you don't make is the best one of all.

Trust Your Intuition

"I just knew without thinking. Something inside told me to do it. It was the right thing to do," said high school baseball coach Frank Russell after he gave the green light to his speedy center fielder to steal third base in extra innings of a league championship game. On the steal, the throw from the catcher skipped by the third baseman and rolled into the outfield. The speedster raced to home and slid in safely under the tag for the winning run. Russell was using what many coaches possess and need to trust to be successful: *intuition,* real knowledge based on wisdom from athletic and coaching experience. It is direct knowing without the conscious use of reason or thought. Intuition is more than just pure chance or simply a hunch. This "gut feeling" comes from the many hours of studying and planning how to address a situation and from learning from past experiences or situations. Russell didn't

The intuition of seasoned coaches such as Tommy Lasorda can be developed through experience, awareness, and trust.

have much time to think—had he hesitated, it would have been too late. Good coaches win games and championships because they trust their inner sense of what's right without question. And by trusting your intuition, you teach athletes to do the same.

Those coaches who have a "feel" for making the right decision at the right time are more than lucky. They are gifted with a special understanding of their sport and the many factors specific to the circumstances at hand. How can you creatively develop this intuitiveness in your own program? Begin to trust yourself and your experiences in your sport and in working with your athletes. Start by keeping a journal in which you note decisions you've made based on your simply knowing it was "the right thing to do."

Ultimately, when you have years of using your cognition (what the mind knows to be right) with your intuition (what the heart knows to be right), you are in a position to know the truth about certain situations.

Here's an example to prove this point. Coaches train athletes to respond quickly, without thought, in specific situations. For instance, with no outs, bases loaded, and a ground ball to first, there's no doubt how the play will evolve for the first baseman. Throw home for the force-out, back to first—a quick response that has become intuitive from experience.

You can be much more effective when you act according to the laws of your inner self and trust the inherent correctness of your intuition when solving problems, making decisions, and answering questions. Ask yourself *What feels right?* and give the answer some weight. You can combine this with input from others or take more time to analyze the situation. Many of us needlessly search for solutions to problems by going "outside" ourselves and following ways that simply do not feel right. Perhaps you've been coaching your sport for a number of years, and before that you were an athlete. You really do know how to act in most situations; you need to trust and follow that inner voice and see for yourself that you knew all along what was the right thing to do. It takes courage and practice, but the payoffs will reward you.

When you stop second-guessing yourself, you become more confident, consistent, and happier with your work and relationships with the athletes. Doing what *feels* right is as important as doing what you rationally *know* may be right. We need to take both aspects—intuitive feelings and rational thought—into account when making our decisions. If our intuitive sense seems stronger, give more attention to it. Being adaptable to situations and open to change is also part of intuitiveness. When you get the chance to intuitively act on something in coaching, take the risk and follow your innate wisdom and notice the outcome. This behavior requires practice; in time you'll discover its value.

Missy Meharg, University of Maryland field hockey coach, intuitively knew before a key match between her team and the University of Virginia that her starting goalie would play the entire game unless her team orchestrated a lead of at least four goals, at which time her backup goalie would enter to get some experience.

With the score 3-0 and two-thirds of the game over, she went against her instincts and substituted the backup in hopes of pleasing that athlete by doing so. Virginia scored two quick goals and was back in the game. The contest came down to a penalty shot for Virginia with no time remaining on the clock. Fortunately for Missy, they missed, and Maryland escaped with a narrow victory. Coach Meharg admitted to me in our postgame wrap-up that she made a huge mistake by not listening to her intuitive sense, what she felt was right. She substituted, against her intuition, only to please an unhappy athlete rather than staying with her plan of beating Virginia decisively and then going with the new goalie. She said she'd do it differently in the future. Missy demonstrates that we all make mistakes and we can learn from ourselves. This was a snippet in her illustrious career and she's a better coach because of it.

Coach Missy Meharg practices the fine art of balancing intellect and instinct in making decisions.

There has been a strong movement in corporate circles to rely on the heart in the decision-making process behind multimillion-dollar business deals. Intuitive management is encouraged by CEOs who understand the value of inner wisdom as a guiding force. The same inner wisdom is valuable for coaches as well. You are probably a warehouse of athletic knowledge; just remember that and trust your wisdom. Use it often and pair it with a look at the data and the results. Train yourself through experimentation to become more confident and less fearful. Start out with smaller decisions and go with what you feel to be right. Gradually work up to those you believe are the bigger decisions and notice the confidence you feel.

Do what feels right. When you second-guess yourself, you hesitate, lose confidence, and become less effective as a leader.

Cindy Timchal, coach of the University of Maryland women's lacrosse team, has had to train herself in trusting her intuitive coaching. For example, her team was on a winning streak of seven games (7-0) to start the season, and the team had just beaten archrival Virginia. Cindy was thrilled with their level of play, yet seemed concerned about their next opponent. She said to me, "What about *Dartmouth?*" as if she needed something new and different. I responded, "What *about* Dartmouth?" She laughed because she recognized there was nothing new to do; rather, the team needed to focus on how they could execute a perfect game just as they had been doing. It became a standing joke with us, but the interaction helped her to see that she needed to trust what she already knew, and that was to focus on her own team's preparation. Let Dartmouth compile 18 pages of scouting reports on their opponents; Maryland would concentrate on themselves. Cindy had those old voices in her head (that all coaches have) telling her to worry about the opponent rather than to prepare her team.

One way to train yourself to rely on your own intuition is to use a tactic that a coach of a junior college soccer team uses. He creates in his mind a "personal coach" he consults whenever he has questions, problems, or decisions to make. He's modeled this "teacher in the mind" from his true mentor, an NCAA Division I coach who lives three thousand miles away. In a relaxed state, he imagines asking his coach advice about a particular situation and waits for the answer. This "wise teacher" sheds light on the problem area, and the coach finds it easier to take action. In reality, of course, this "voice" is really his own inner voice, a reflection of what he is feeling, his best intuitive judgment. This strategy can work quite well, especially when you have the luxury of taking some time to make decisions.

Consider setting aside a specific time each day to quietly relax and listen to what your intuition is telling you. Ask these questions:

- What do I need to do?
- What do I need to know?
- How do I need to act in this situation?

Let your mind speak its wisdom. Create moments to reflect on what you intuitively know is right, what feels good.

Too many times I find myself eager to overanalyze and think excessively about opponents. Scouting and data collection are important, but to what extent does such analysis interfere with the natural flow of preparation and simply competing? I believe that many successful coaches create a balance between scouting and playing their game. However, some coaches have a less balanced style and still see success. John Wooden rarely used his time scouting the other team. He believed it interfered with his team's preparation to play their best and to focus on what they could do. Yet Roy Williams, head basketball coach at Kansas, gathers volumes on his opponents, and who could argue with his track record? It seems to work for Roy.

Don't overanalyze situations.
Doing so blocks the natural rhythm and
flow of playing the game.

Do not be concerned that others may scrutinize you if your feeling turns out to be incorrect. First of all, you know what goes into making a decision; and second, you probably will be right more often by using your gut because it's real knowledge based on your experience. If you are a younger, inexperienced coach, use older head coaches as mentors and begin to build your expertise through learning by doing. In time, your confidence using intuitive wisdom will begin to get stronger.

Back at Maryland, I know that Cindy is more than happy to let her opponents try to figure out how to beat her team. She spends most of her time on enhancing her own team's particular style of play. She focuses on what Maryland can control—the execution of excellent lacrosse. It took her time to trust this, but now she's willing to let the game flow, to play with intuitive spirit and relaxed intensity.

Guide for Growth

Remember our discussion in chapter 3 about providing an atmosphere of service for your athletes, an environment that allows them to grow as athletes and individuals? You can further apply that attitude of service in the way you encourage athletes to think for themselves and to take responsibility for their actions.

Ask the Right Questions

Have you considered the power of a question in your coach's arsenal? Properly phrased and expertly timed questions lead others to the so-called "promised land." For example, observing a masterful basketball practice session with Coach Mike Krzyzewski at Duke University, I noticed how his use of questions helps him to teach athletes to grow and expand. When a player makes a mistake, he doesn't explode and scream about what should be done and how. Instead, he blows his whistle and quietly asks, "Now, Chris [Carrawell], what do you need to do when Elton [Brand] comes to the elbow?" Chris reflects and sees his error, immediately correcting it. Coach K then asks, "What would happen if you went left in this situation?" Chris answers, and Coach says, "That's right, Chris." Then he opens it up to the team: "Does everyone see that? Good." And play continues. In a calm, respectful, guiding tone, Coach K guides the athletes to help him make his point and the entire team follows, feeling they are doing it themselves, for themselves. He stays in the background and facilitates the players' development, and the beauty of it all is that this essentially goes unnoticed. That is, until his team's record reflects his ability to effectively lead his team.

Avoid getting caught in the trap of always telling athletes what to do. Look for opportunities to use questions to lead and guide. Ask them "How could you do that better? What can you do to better this? What are some of the options in this case? What happens when you do [name a behavior]?" Note that this guidance occurs *during* practice, while the error or mistake is being made, so that self-correction and self-reflection can take place immediately, not after the fact.

When questions fail to get the athlete to create movement, try using suggestions. For example, say to a player, "You know, you might want to try _____ or do _____." Or "When I find myself in this situation, I like to _____. You may want to think about it." Or "It would be a good idea if we, as a team, would _____." This is a softer yet stronger approach to getting things to happen. And the result is greater cooperation with a sense of personal accountability.

Delegate Responsibility to the Team

Another way to guide athletes is to delegate—give them the opportunity to create self-responsibility. I have always struggled with effective delegation myself, because I tend to believe that I'm the best person to do the job. Wanting to have more of a say, I take on the entire project and then become resentful of all that I "have" to do. I've come to learn, however, that I am more effective in my work when I delegate to others and let go of the need to have all things done my way. Rather than telling your athletes to do something, suggest to them "I need this to be done, and I'd appreciate someone stepping up to do the job." Emphasize the point that the individuals—athletes, coaches, staff, everyone—need to work together for the greater good of the team.

Delegate, delegate, delegate:
*three ways to get athletes to take responsibility
for their team and to help coaches let go
of the need to control everything.*

This approach has worked quite well with several of the coaches I know. Quin Snyder does not hesitate to delegate. Trainers, managers, assistant coaches, and administrative assistants all take on work not necessarily outlined in the job description. This not only helps to get the job done more effectively, it creates more harmony and unity in the program. For example, Quin's right-hand man, Lee Rashman, has the job of picking me up from the airport on my visits to Columbia. Lee and I get two uninterrupted hours or more to discuss the program, the needs I should address, and the state of the "heart" of Missouri basketball. Lee provides me with his valuable insights, which help me to be more prepared when I arrive.

- Rules protect us from chaos and keep us aligned with our goals and purpose.

- I am a creative, decisive coach capable of making the best decision for all involved. My ability to be clearly decisive makes me a more effective leader.

- I trust the inherent correctness of my wise, intuitive self. I follow my heart, what I deeply know to be true, and consider all other data presented to me.

- I make suggestions rather than shout orders. Because of this, my athletes are more willing to cooperate and be accountable.

- I choose to guide my athletes rather than control everything they do. When I guide, I give the players the opportunity to explore the limitless boundaries of their potential.

The job of a coach is to lead the team and to develop a team of leaders. By setting boundaries, making decisions, respecting intuition as well as hard data, and providing guidance, you enable your athletes to focus on being the best they can be. As they follow you, they will learn to lead themselves and their teammates.

6

Developing Discipline

All great performances and breakthroughs are the result of working through adversity, sacrificing, and suffering.

To provide creative guidance, a coach must model desire and discipline. *Desire* is the willingness to do all that it takes to get a job done; *discipline* is reflected in the drive and actions you do consistently in pursuit of fulfilling this desire in a positive learning and training environment. An athlete must truly desire to reach greater heights before she can learn to be disciplined to do so. Coaches can ignite a fire of desire in their athletes if the athletes are open to it.

Determining Desire

Most athletes would like to experience greatness, to be successful in their sport. Yet only those who truly desire it and are willing to do all that it takes to achieve their highest possible level of performance become champions. An athlete with a desire to achieve would never ask, "Coach, I want to, but what will it take?" Rather, the athlete with desire would say, "Coach, I want to—tell me what I need to do now." The latter comment shows deep desire and passion, the willingness to suffer, sacrifice, and serve on the road to realizing one's full potential.

At the beginning of each season (and perhaps periodically throughout the season) ask your athletes, "What is worth the sacrifice for you? What does it mean to suffer in the process of getting better?" The answers to these questions will help you discern their willingness to do the job. Give them a vision of the sacrifice and suffering they will need to accept to be better athletes. An athlete may need to play a different role on the team with less playing time, or give up some social life, or start working out twice a day. Once athletes become aware of the specific sacrifices or changes they need to make to be more disciplined, they may decide that they don't really have the deep desire needed to go forward.

Many good athletes do not want to go the distance; they are satisfied with their present level of achievement. I see this often with complacent high school and collegiate stars who are content to be really good as opposed to working harder to be the best they can be. They are not willing to give up certain things they enjoy, and this reluctance proves what their real desire is. You can assist some of these athletes by helping them find ways to best manage their time so that they can minimize sacrificing areas of their life that make them more balanced. Yet regardless of what you do to assist athletes, some will see no reason to sacrifice, suffer, or challenge themselves any more than they are already doing; they are content to remain in their comfort zone.

All great performances, breakthroughs, and achievements are the result of some form of pain (physical, mental, emotional, spiritual), adversity, sacrifice, and suffering. Yet the fun of full extension to reach one's goals makes it all worthwhile. Roger Bannister, the first person to run a four-minute mile, claimed that in "the joy of going all out, I forgot my pain." His necessary suffering was overshadowed by his pleasure in reaching his goal.

For athletes to develop the desire to maximize their potential, their goals must be meaningful.

Balance is an essential aspect of discipline in athletics. Disciplined athletes need to be able to discern injury or acute pain from the pain of fatigue and hard work. Part of being disciplined as an athlete (and as a coach training athletes) is to realize that recovery or rest is a vital part of this training, and in fact is necessary to maximize the effects of hard training and to prevent overtraining or overuse injuries. Athletes must not be permitted to devote themselves to their sport to the extent of excluding attention to the rest of their lives. They still have to do their homework or make a living, and they need to make some time for social outlets.

Unbalanced desire can even lure an athlete to harm her body (in such ways as using banned substances or engaging in questionable eating practices). If you see signs of unhealthy behavior, speak with your athlete about the importance of maintaining disciplined balance between athletics and life. If necessary, sit down with her and help her draw up a schedule that reflects desire in sport and attention to details in her personal life. Help athletes understand that desire to accomplish something is not simply measured in terms of the volume of work. As a coach, you determine the quality of work, and athletes' desire determines their willingness to follow through.

Many of the coaches and athletes I have worked with demonstrate their willingness to enter a zone of discomfort to become better. They are in awe of the famed "marathon monks" in Japan who endure great pain to achieve their "championship," a state of complete awareness and sensitivity to life. These Buddhist monks arise every day at 1:30 A.M. in the subzero cold, high in the mountains. Dressed in nothing but a white robe and sandals, they run up and down the steep slopes for 19 to 52 miles for a total of one thousand days over a seven-year span.

In Zen Buddhism, white is the color associated with death—so if a monk happens to not make the run one day, he's prepared for the outcome. It's a dishonor to fail to complete the run, so each monk also carries a small sword with him so that he can commit suicide if he gives up. After about seven hundred miles, the monks engage in a nine-day fast without food, water, or sleep—a fast longer that most people believe to be possible. The training transforms the survivors, making them more grateful for life, full of energy, aware of and sensitive to life, able to hear the sound of ashes falling from a burning stick of incense. They are radiant with a vision of ultimate existence. Their suffering, sacrifice, and ability to face adversity opens them up to their spiritual greatness. The marathon monks talk about the joy they experience in having endured such a journey.

When athletes hear this story, most perk up and gain new perspective on suffering to achieve their greatness. The story demonstrates that there can be joy in the difficult journey. Clearly, coaches do not ask athletes to take on the adversity of these monks, nor does anyone expect an athlete to relate to such extremes. However, athletes often must push the envelope in other ways. When you talk to your athletes about the concept of sacrifice or suffering, remember to ask the questions we discussed previously: "What is suffering for you in athletics, school, and life?" For some athletes, having "diminished" roles such as fewer playing minutes could be a kind of suffering. The physical pain of pushing one's limits and subsequent fatigue could be another form of suffering.

To improve, athletes may need to consider arriving early for practice or staying late afterward. In order to do this, however, they will first need to have a deep desire to improve. We need to realize the importance of this before pinpointing how they will put this desire into action. Losing and making mistakes is painful; you can count on suffering because of unexpected setbacks. For student-athletes, grades or social life could take a hit when they follow their desires to develop their full athletic potential. Give the athletes a chance to explore the ways they may need to sacrifice and suffer. As their coach, you can provide the opportunity to take it on and help guide them through it.

Nurturing Discipline

The word *discipline* is from the Latin word *disciplinus,* which means "disciple," "follower," or "learner." Players follow best and learn the most when treated with respect through guidance and fair, firm rules. As a coach, you discipline your athletes to help them learn self-control, character, and a sense of order, and to improve their sport skills and physical and behavioral conditioning. Although the term *discipline* is often used synonymously with *obedience* or *punishment,* I prefer to use it in the context of control, order, learning, and training, as a concept that motivates (for example, I discipline myself to write each day). I use the term *punishment* to refer to what happens as a consequence of not fulfilling an obligation or of breaking a rule. With that understanding, it is more fruitful to discuss how you can creatively teach sport discipline to your athletes and teams to help them learn and grow as people and players.

The type of discipline needed for athletic excellence is the same kind that drove Mike Bibby to practice 500 shots a day, every day, for two months during the summer before his sophomore year at the University of Arizona. He developed self-control and a deadly three-pointer and proceeded to shoot the lights out that season on his way to becoming a high first-round NBA draft pick.

Is it any coincidence that perhaps the two best football players of all time, Walter Payton and Jerry Rice, were also among the most disciplined athletes in their sport? The stories of their tortuous off-season workouts, pushing their bodies to the limits in sweltering summer heat and humidity, up steep inclines that even mountain goats would hesitate to climb, are now legends. Why do this to themselves? Both had already made millions of dollars in salary and endorsements. Both had secured a place as certain first-ballot inductees in football's hall of fame when they became eligible. Both had set numerous records for players at their respective positions, running back and wide receiver.

But Payton and Rice were different—just as hurdle legend Edwin Moses, wrestling great Dan Gable, and track star Jackie Joyner Kersee were different. Ordinary physical and mental thresholds do not apply. Their goals were more than simply to "just win, baby," as Oakland Raiders' owner Al Davis puts it; they wanted to dominate, to be the best of all time, and they committed totally to achieving that aim.

Of that group, Gable is the only one who tried his hand at coaching. As head coach at the University of Iowa, he demanded just as much of himself as a coach as he did as an athlete, when he lost only one match in his entire high school and college wrestling career and claimed a gold medal in the 1972 Olympics without allowing his opponents a single point. The results were similarly superb. His Hawkeye teams claimed 15 NCAA Championships in his 21-year coaching career. No secrets to their success. Year in and year out, they were the hardest working and hungriest team, following the lead of their coach.

Discipline is a learning process that helps athletes to develop drive, self-control, order, character, and skill.

Disciplined athletes spend optimal amounts of time practicing, and the outcome is greater self-control not only in sport, but in all aspects of life. A good example of an athlete who regained his self-discipline to rise to the top of his sport is tennis star Andre Agassi. In 1998, Agassi was ranked 141st in the world. His coach told him the only way he was going to turn around his career was to make a commitment to condition his body and dedicate his mind so that he could get back to the elite level.

Agassi voluntarily took part of the year and played the challenger circuit—akin to a baseball player going down to the minor leagues—to work on his game. His renewed mental and physical dedication led to his impressive 1999 string in which he won the French Open, lost in the finals at Wimbledon, and won the U.S. Open to become the first-ranked player in the world.

To successfully and creatively hone discipline, athletes and coaches need to focus on not just conditioning and skills training

A renewed commitment to physical and mental discipline put Andre Agassi back in top form.

but also on making more disciplined lifestyle choices in terms of nutrition, sleep, staying away from alcohol and drugs, and using meditation and visualization as part of a daily conditioning routine. Moreover, athletes and their coaches need to discipline themselves to adhere to a patient and balanced approach to training.

Choosing a Disciplined Lifestyle

For all athletes, discipline means control—being focused, attentive, assertive, and aware, on and off the court. The discipline to carry over into one's lifestyle the behaviors necessary to reach one's athletic potential is something that athletes can learn. All the coaches I work with teach and train their athletes to be disciplined in body, mind, and spirit.

One of the most important ways they do this is to help athletes control their own health, awareness, and energy levels on and off the playing field with good nutrition. Whether you have a certified clinical nutritionist available or must seek out other resources, it's important to help athletes see that making good nutritional choices is a part of being a disciplined athlete.

Another good way to help athletes be disciplined in body, mind, and spirit is to expose them to the practice of meditation and visualization on a regular basis. This helps them to be more focused, aware, and attentive, three ingredients necessary for being disciplined. The teams I have worked with have excellent discipline at practice, during games, and away from sport. The coaches attribute this to their ritual of meditation and visualization on a daily basis.

Naturally, for learning to occur, there needs to be an environment in which respect, communication, acceptance, trust, and compassion exist, qualities emphasized in previous chapters. Without this type of environment athletes will resist any attempt at discipline and will resent it when it is forced on them. Given the proper environment, accept that it takes time to create disciplined athletes. For some, it could be almost immediate. For others, it could take a year or more. Keep in mind the cumulative benefits of physical, mental, and experiential training over years. If you try to rush the process, you will end up controlling your athletes because that's easier than taking the time to teach self-discipline. Taking the time to teach self-discipline builds the structure within which solid teams can be created.

Perfecting Patience and Timing

A wise, creative coach shared with me an expression that awakened me to the importance of timing in all of our endeavors: *Right things happen when the time is right.*

In my attempt to become a national-class runner, I overtrained until I became severely injured. I wasn't patient, and it took almost a year before I regained my original level of fitness. If I had gone at the task more slowly, I could have, paradoxically, reached my goal of becoming a national-class runner much sooner. The body needs time to get conditioned to new, demanding physical regimens. Experience and subsequent wisdom take time also. Remember the story about the race between the tortoise and the hare? By consistent, deliberate, steady, slow movement, the tortoise arrived at the finish line sooner than the quicker yet more spastic, inconsistent, and fatigued hare. We can't force things to happen before their time.

I now understand the importance of *wait training;* that is, training yourself to wait for the right time. As a coach, this is the wisdom of knowing what you have to work with and giving an athlete the time to blossom. This wisdom becomes part of your best intuitive sense, which we discussed in chapter 5. Planning, preparing, and discussing training and goals with the athlete or team can facilitate the wait training process.

So many athletes get hung up on making rapid, big gains. I've been that way most of my life—"I want it now! I don't want to wait!" Coaches who have experienced success, who have made it to the top, all tell me that it took time. Duke's Mike Krzyzewski needed at least three building years before he began to experience victory. Dean Smith had a rough beginning those first few years at North Carolina. He held out and was patient, knowing he would recruit good athletes and turn things around in a short time.

Coaches especially see the futility in rushing the clock when their athletes are injured. Frustrated, annoyed, and angry, many athletes and coaches decide to make comebacks before the body is healed, only to experience further injury and greater frustration. It's not easy as a coach to have injured athletes, especially when you rely on each player's contribution to the team effort, but it's necessary for the coach and team to adjust and adapt to the crisis. Often something good can come of it. Athletes can grow in appreciation of their stature; they can become more excited to compete when they heal; they can regain a positive perspective and see the futility in always forcing and pressuring themselves.

A freshman athlete at Duke University asked her coach how long it would take to earn a starting role on their talent-laden team. The coach reassured the athlete that if she trained properly and listened to the staff, it would take another year. Disappointed, the athlete replied that she didn't want to wait that long and asked how long it would take if she worked harder and practiced twice the time. The astute coach quickly responded, "In that case, it could take two to three years." The coach knew that trying to hasten the process would make injury more likely. Also, it simply takes time to adjust to a higher level of play, and the coach wanted to be sure the athlete didn't get discouraged, burned out, or disillusioned. She encouraged her to slow down, relax, and stay focused on the process of improving and getting stronger and fitter. As a sophomore, the athlete became a strong contributor in a starting role.

Reassure your athletes that too-rapid growth and advancement can be detrimental to their goals. Individual and team potential blossom gradually. Tell them that snags and obstacles are going to happen. Let them know the dangers of comparing their own progress to that of others.

Rapid advancement is contrary to a natural flow.
Growth takes time.

Have you noticed how there's a natural flow to most events, contests, and performances in sports? Encourage your athletes to take notice of their energy, fatigue, soreness, staleness, spurts, plateaus, slumps, enthusiasm, and burnout. I encourage coaches to have their athletes keep training logs; these diaries help athletes keep track of how they feel physically, mentally, emotionally, and spiritually following certain practices and competitive events. With this information, an athlete can begin to understand the relationship between feelings and performance, and the impact of those feelings on a particular performance. Having this data likewise allows you to evaluate a situation and make good decisions about training your athletes. Learning from a training log can take a month or more, but before long, the athlete will find it to be a comforting reminder and tool for determining his level of performance. Crucial items an athlete should record in a training and performance log include the following:

- Date and time of workout or competition
- Components of workout or competition ("30-minute warm-up jog, line drills"; "Game against Red Devils"; or "Swam 100 butterfly and back in 200 medley relay")
- Mental feelings during workout or competition ("Wasn't into it"; "Felt in the groove"; or "Was distracted by my biology test score")
- Physical feelings during workout or competition ("Felt strong and fluid throughout my race"; "The team's passing was better than ever"; or "Noticed some soreness in my left hamstring after the half")

Athletes can add other details to the log, such as things they ate that day, how many hours of sleep they got, or stresses that might be happening in their lives. A log can provide valuable information for the athlete to use in the future when looking for patterns that may be contributing to a turnaround, an injury, or a breakthrough in performance. When possible, I encourage coaches to review their athletes' logs with them to help them both learn what has gotten the athlete back on track and to help them begin to make any necessary adaptations to training.

The element of timing or flow also plays a big role during a competition. Some teams race through a game when all they need to do is to slow down and let the game come to them. Your attack at any point can be strategically determined by time. For example, notice when the opposition's intensity slacks off; an opening occurs and it becomes time to attack. When you see a gap, go forward; when you see it fill up, withdraw. When you are tired or feel insufficient, go on the defensive; when you feel strong and feisty, attack with an offense. Train your athletes to be in the present moment and notice the element of timing and flow, and they will learn to respond appropriately. During practice, judiciously use your whistle whenever you can to stop the action and point out how patience could have led to greater opportunities or how timing could have helped the play to evolve more effectively.

Look for ways to use timing to strategize.
If there's an opening, attack.

Patience enables all of us to stay calmly focused and to enjoy the time it takes for the vision to unfold. By being patient, your athletes increase the chances of getting what they work for. Most things in life happen not when you think they should, but when the time is right.

Bringing About Balance

Our minds are powerful instruments, capable of pushing us to levels of performance we never knew were possible. Yet these same minds often push our bodies beyond what they can handle. This is called *excessiveness,* and athletes tend to be excessive, thinking that more training, stricter diets, and so forth will always translate to better performance. In our passion for our sport, we constantly walk the fine line between enthusiasm and excessiveness.

A national-class cyclist was getting stellar results from her training program. She hoped to make the Olympic team and thought about how much better her chances would be if she upped her mileage and intensity. She followed the reasoning that "more is better" and seriously injured her lower back, blowing her chances to make the team. The temptation to increase her effort was enticing, but in the end, self-destructive. The difference between optimal training and overtraining can force an athlete to walk a fine line between being in top form or getting injured. Always be on the alert for such excessiveness. Often it is an experiment, but all athletes have their breaking points and must pay attention to the early warnings of overtraining: ongoing fatigue, irritability, disruptive sleep patterns, and small aches that don't seem to go away quickly.

A coach's most effective role is to modulate the enthusiasm of athletes and staff toward excess; this will create more success. A smarter approach to continuous, steady performance improvement is balance and moderation. Do not confuse moderation with slacking off. Moderation is a balance between serious, definitive, quality work and resting the body to fuel it for the next workout. By balancing hard work with adequate recovery, athletes can have higher-quality workouts and thus make these sessions more beneficial to their overall conditioning. A good rule of thumb is to always follow a demanding workout with an easier training session. "Easy" is subjective and must be determined according to the fitness level of the athlete.

Many coaches are beginning to understand the wisdom of moderation. They have discovered that they can train their athletes diligently and consistently, yet moderately, without a loss in conditioning or skill level. Actually, several coaches I've worked with have seen bigger strides by cutting back the training regimen of their athletes. Instead of her traditional three-hour practice sessions, one winning NCAA coach now conducts two-hour sessions and claims that her athletes have less fatigue, more vitality and enthusiasm, fewer injuries, greater focus at practice, and a greater willingness to give it their all on the practice field. Thus the result is better overall practice quality. Her athletes are actually more rested for the game and less tired in the closing minutes of the competition.

I compare this approach with that of coaches who fear that others will catch up if they don't keep the pressure on the athletes. One coach had his team practice twice a day for 18 straight days only to discover an enormous drop in focus, enthusiasm, and energy in his players. The team was on the brink of mutiny when the coach wisely reevaluated the excessive training schedule and began to realize that less practice could optimize his team's fitness. The spirit of the team quickly reversed with a new policy of moderation coupled with intensity. Their bodies started to recuperate and get stronger in this "stress, then rest" environment. They are not only experiencing the physical benefits of moderation, but the spiritual as well; their morale and enthusiasm have never been stronger.

Current research in the area of excessive training in swimming has indicated that swimming programs with high intensity or volume (over 10,000 meters per day) do not appear to produce additional improvement in conditioning or performance over more moderate training volumes. Furthermore, excessive training can lead to a chronic state of fatigue associated with muscle glycogen depletion. Studies conducted thus far reveal no scientific evidence that double daily training sessions enhance fitness and performance more than single daily sessions. Large training volume prepares the athlete to tolerate high volume, but does little to benefit performance. It appears that training volume could be reduced significantly, perhaps by as much as half in some sports, without losing any conditioning and with less risk of athlete burnout, overload, and injury.

Moderation plus intensity is a hedge against fatigue, illness, injury, and burnout. The level of intensity sets the stage for improvement.

I like to compare a good team to good music. There's great harmony throughout both, and rest is an integral part of their greatness. What makes truly good music is the space or pause between the notes. In the same way, achieving peak fitness through training is the result of optimal rest between workouts. Guide your athletes to higher levels rather than forcing them there. Look for opportunities where moderation might be a better, richer alternative than excessiveness: number of practices, length of practices, or frequency of alternative conditioning techniques such as weights, running, and cross-training.

It's not easy to generate specific, creative ways to achieve the right balance for optimal performance; often it's a trial-and-error experience for each athlete. Experiment by gradually altering your normal routines. Do this especially when your athletes seem to be having more injury or illness than usual. Notice how an athlete's motivation improves; excitement, joy, enthusiasm, and satisfaction return when you make choices toward moderation instead of excessiveness.

There is a delicate balance between enough and too much. Again, it's experimental. Be on the lookout for signs of overtraining. The following are some indicators of overdoing it:

- Any radical change in sleep patterns resulting in too much or not enough sleep

- Changes in food consumption, such as eating too much or not enough
- Accidents, injury, and sickness occurring more often than usual
- Constant fatigue
- Irritable or cranky mood in athletes who are normally easy-going
- Difficulty in maintaining attention or focus

If you notice any of these indicators, ask an athlete what she feels is going on. For example, you could say, "I notice that you've been having a hard time focusing at practice; what do you suppose is happening? How is your training going?" You might suggest that she review her training log for insight. Always be on the lookout for signs of overtraining and make adjustments to training as needed.

I strongly recommend that you read the most pertinent training sources available in your sport and continue to educate yourself on training and new ways to achieve results. Many coaches rightly rely on their vast experience and use workouts that work year after year with athletes—but coaches should never stop learning. Use some of the resources in the references and resources of this book, or seek out new resources on the Internet. Coaching is exciting and challenging because there is always something to learn. That's what makes it such an attractive profession. Challenge yourself to be the best you can be, and you will have more reason to ask the same of your athletes.

One last point. It becomes obvious to most of us that there is a time for everything, including focusing more exclusively on one's training and sport. This is not a contradiction to what I've been espousing. Clearly there may be times when devoting your time to one aspect of life is necessary to get the job done. For example, if a team is in position to challenge for a championship, they may need to become totally consumed by their sport. We're talking about a relatively short period in life, one in which complete devotion may result in victory. So, we get out of balance, tunnel our vision, and go for the gusto. After you have given your all, you rest assured that you can recuperate when the season has finished and return to a more moderate regimen.

Focusing on the Conditioning Payoff

Athletes need discipline in three specific areas of conditioning: *physical, skill,* and *behavioral.* For athletes other than those who have a strong work ethic coupled with desire to improve, disciplining athletes to improve their physical conditioning can be a difficult proposition at best. This is especially true of players in sports that rely more heavily on skills training, because they may not see the direct benefits of physical conditioning. They may believe that it takes away from their skill development practice time. Getting players to push their bodies to breakthrough levels is agonizing for any coach. Athletes may not desire to be the greatest they can be and may sabotage or cut corners in the training regimen. Satisfied with the levels they have already attained, they are unwilling to enter into the discomfort zone. Many athletes become complacent and refuse to sacrifice or suffer to raise the bar.

With desire, an athlete will do all that it takes to realize full potential. In his book *Values of the Game,* Bill Bradley says, "I used to hate getting into shape . . . . After six weeks of agony . . . the pain began to diminish and the muscles started to come around . . . . When the body is honed, you can run your opponents round and round" (page 32). Physically conditioned athletes force their opponents to crack, to give up.

Athletes who cut corners not only jeopardize their own conditioning, but also negatively influence their team. Liz Tchou, head coach of women's field hockey at Duke University, had an athlete who did her best to avoid the team's ritual two-mile run in preseason training. She would complain and drag her feet, running last every time. She would talk about her sore muscles and her fatigue. She even missed a few sessions. Liz noticed the overall impact of this attitude on the team's preseason morale. The negative emotional virus started to spread. Other athletes began behaving in similar ways. Those who were really into it began to get disgusted with those who were sabotaging the program, and this led to disharmony and poor team bonding. Fortunately, Coach Tchou took action to reverse the problem. She gave a gentle ultimatum—choose to join the journey of improvement (which training is a key part of) or leave the team. The athlete, therefore, was responsible for her fate. She began to realize that there were improvements to be gained and decided to come back to the team with a new frame of heart. This helped pull the whole team together.

There are some other ideas you can use to help encourage and motivate athletes to take advantage of their physical conditioning. Keeping a log and monitoring such assessments as strength or fitness tests can motivate athletes. Perhaps a grid chart that plots days of the week on one axis and certain activities—such as running, weight training, stretching, skill practice, and so on—on the other would be helpful. It is quite encouraging to see the checkmarks accumulate.

Another activity that could help athletes expand their conditioning is to ask them to answer these questions in their off season—or, as I like to call it, their *developmental season,* since the athletes are not necessarily "off" from keeping up their basic fitness.

1. How fit would you like to be when you return?
2. What will it take to be there?
3. What are you willing to commit to doing in order to prove you are serious about becoming closer to your ideal self?

Have athletes record their answers to these questions and pass them out to each team member. This makes each athlete accountable and shows the team the level of commitment each member has to his teammates. Provide guidance and encouragement where needed in this stage. One way to do this is to create a "laundry list" of items that athletes can choose from, things that will be worthwhile for them to do during their developmental season. For example, specific skill work, weight training, endurance building, focusing on consistency in training, and competing a few times for fun are but a few areas that athletes can focus on. Let the athletes be responsible to one another and trust that if they truly wish to get there, they will do the work. If they don't, there is nothing you can do to change this desire.

Skill development as a discipline may be a little easier for a coach to create than overall conditioning. As Bill Bradley says, the way to become a shooter is by shooting. We need to remember, however, that without determination, desire, a will to improve, and a good old-fashioned work ethic, discipline in skill development is usually nonexistent. An athlete has to want to do this; a coach simply provides the structure. Again, all major break-throughs in sports are the by-product of the sacrifice and suffering that athletes are willing to absorb. Constantly remind your athletes of the importance of this concept. Ask them if they are willing to sacrifice—come early, stay late, work out in the off season. If they act on this, it will indicate their level of commitment and discipline necessary for optimal performance.

Building Better Habits

Behavioral conditioning comes about as a result of the team's established guidelines and rules, a way of disciplining the athletes into the system. It is based on the team's objectives and goals. These guidelines and rules nudge the players toward self-control, with desire and determination as essential ingredients in this process.

Athletes must be taught to be disciplined. This process begins with you; you model discipline by demonstrating your willingness to be disciplined in your work and life. How can we ask our athletes to take on a conditioning program while we are out of shape? Learn how much more disciplined athletes become when you choose to be fit by exercising on a regular basis. Notice how athletes behave in pressure situations when you model constructive behaviors under pressure.

Reinforce Discipline

You can teach discipline by rewarding certain behaviors. For example, you may notice an athlete listening intently to you during practice; tell the athlete how you appreciate that. When an athlete comes early to practice, point it out to the entire team. Anything athletes do that shows more discipline, be sure to reinforce with a word, a note, or an award for MDP (Most Disciplined Player) of the week. Create categories such as "early to practice," "staying late," and "extra cross-training," and have athletes chart their behaviors.

Of course, be sure to monitor their patterns and prevent any athlete from going overboard. If you notice that an athlete is constantly fatigued or burned out (see overtraining indicators listed on pages 127-128), the athlete may be overdoing it.

Make Discipline Fun

Whether it's conditioning or skill development, look for ways to bring more enjoyment to the equation. Coaches who have well-disciplined teams realize that athletes will be more receptive to hard work if there's some fun involved; they will go the extra mile if they enjoy what they do.

It's important not to confuse fun with goofing off. Coach Timchal at Maryland talks to her national champion lacrosse players about the fun in the execution of a well-thought-out offensive plan. Roger Bannister talked about the joy and fun of going all out, even with the pain. Fun doesn't mean you take the job of training less seriously. Fun is simply toning down the stress, anxiety, and pressure. Fun is why most athletes started doing their sport in the first place!

Find drills or workouts that your athletes can do well, that will be fun for them, especially if you can end a practice with them. Sometimes it's fun for athletes to decide what they'd like to do the last 20 minutes of practice. An unstructured, unsupervised scrimmage works well for many game sports. Deryk Snelling, Olympic coach of the British men's and women's swim teams, likes to hold floor hockey games before morning practices.

> I like to mix the men and women on the teams. It can be highly competitive and allows the women to be as aggressive as they wish, checking and charging, whereas the men must not make aggressive contact with the women or retaliate in any way. In this way the women can give free reign to their aggression, and the fact that the men have to control theirs encourages them to develop more subtle skills and self-control, so everyone benefits. These games are so popular that it is not unusual for the athletes to turn up more than 20 minutes early for a 6:00 A.M. workout so that they can enjoy warm-ups, shooting skills, etc. Some will even ask to come in for a game on their day off. The team goes into swim workout charged, excited, and really positive, which is especially important as morning workouts should be just as good as afternoon sessions. In top-class competition so many swimmers don't make finals because they are not conditioned to go fast in the morning heats.

Advantages to the coach are excellent attendance, happy early morning start, development of teamwork, and a great warm-up. It gives me a realistic expectation of what to expect and often a better sense of how to work with each swimmer when we get into the pool. It also gives me an opportunity to evaluate assertiveness, self-control, attitude, and quickness—altogether a great way to start your day.

Athletes are happy to work hard if they're having fun.

Another way Coach Snelling likes to add variety to his workouts while still encouraging discipline is to bring in world-class coaches and athletes from other sports to speak to his team. He notes in *The Swim Coaching Bible:*

> Every sport has its own characteristics, with its distinct strengths and weaknesses, that we can study, adapt, and incorporate into our training methods. Olympic gymnastics coaches know how to develop strength and flexibility, particularly relative to pound for pound of body weight, and track coaches are particularly adept at developing speed, endurance, and explosive power.
>
> I have a good friend who was the leader of a very successful Mt. Everest climb; he made a presentation to my group outlining their training regimes and how they learned to deal with stress and fear. He told of his own personal trauma when some members of the group were killed on the climb and the team had to decide who would carry on and who would go back down.
>
> On the other end of the scale I have brought in practitioners in the art of transcendental meditation who taught us yoga skills during our workouts. I believe that you should always be looking out for ideas to improve your basic skills, keeping training simple and focused, tough and consistent, and that you should always try to adapt new perspectives and activities into your training plan if and when appropriate (manuscript page 143).

See how you might be able to implement similar ideas, or vary these to apply them to making the discipline of your sport more fun.

Introduce fun into the developmental process.

Make Discipline a Ritual

Another way to teach discipline is through *ritual*. Daily, consistent attention to details disciplines athletes to form a habit. For example, when I work with a team, we have a prepractice and pregame ritual, a routine that helps them to focus and play with a "relaxed intensity." This is a discipline of mind and spirit to help athletes get much more from their time practicing or competing. The ritual takes 8 to 10 minutes and includes meditation to help clear the mind of distracting thoughts, immediately followed by visualization exercises, then concluding with affirmations—strong, positive words that reinforce the images and vision. By doing this ritual on a regular basis, the athletes are reinforcing discipline and feeling the advantages of the routine. They get the message that through such discipline, they perform at higher levels. Warm-up rituals, consistent ways to elevate the excitement, are comforting to players. Postseason awards ceremonies and parties are rituals that foster team bonding and encourage discipline throughout the season.

- I create an environment of mutual respect, communication, acceptance, trust, and compassion. Without this, athletes will resist and resent discipline.

- I am a patient coach, capable of using the element of timing to great advantage. Timing is the essence of great play.

- I search for ways to introduce moderation into the training regimen. When I become less excessive, I open up to greater possibilities.

- I am a well-disciplined coach, capable of creating athletes who enjoy a disciplined approach to discovering their greatness.

Coaches I admire who have mastered the concept of discipline pay attention to the following concepts: respect, cooperation (a two-way process), acceptance, encouragement, and modeling desired attitudes and behaviors. Now that we have established some of the ways to create desire and discipline in our athletes, we are ready to focus in the next chapter on instilling inner strength for extraordinary athletic performance.

7

Instilling Inner Strength

Disciplined athletes are equipped to fully develop inner strength, a quality that enables them to do all it takes to realize their full potential. I notice this quality in many top-flight coaches and national champion athletes I've worked with. These "best of the best" have given me insight into what it takes to be a winner. Although it's important to have some talent, skill, and technical know-how, the true champions are those who have through discipline developed enormous inner strength—commitment, persistence, courage, confidence, and belief in their own limitlessness.

An athlete with *desire* is willing to do all that it takes and is committed to specific strategies to help realize the goal. *Persistence* helps the athlete to continue to work through adversity, setback, or failure. *Courage* enables the athlete to stare fear in the face and take risks, knowing that failure may result. The athlete then establishes a *confidence* in his ability to perform those strategies, knowing that there truly are no limits to what he can achieve.

Duke University's women's basketball team has benefited from such team-wide inner strength. In the 1999 East Regional, Duke wasn't given much of a chance against the talented national champions from the University of Tennessee, a team expected to be in the Final Four. But the fearless, confident, courageous group of hungry Blue Devils from Duke took Tennessee by surprise to win the game. For an entire year prior to this game, the coaching staff and I had worked with these athletes, focusing on the qualities of their inner strength. Each week we had taken some time to talk about the journey to the Final Four. The athletes would specifically define what they were willing to commit to doing each day along the path. By focusing on "in-the-moment" details, such as diving for loose balls, boxing out, or sprinting back on defense every time, they gained confidence in what they could do, rather than focusing on the outcomes or results, things they couldn't control.

Traditionally, sport is seen as a battlefield against an opponent, a clock, a scoreboard. The Blue Devils, however, saw their journey as an arena for their own battles against fear, failure, fatigue, self-doubt, and ego. The athletes' inner strength helped them to understand the importance of winning as a reflection of victory over the inner battles. They wanted to win but showed up to demonstrate how to play courageous, fearless basketball—to simply display their level of greatness.

In this chapter we'll closely examine the qualities that can help your athletes become "inner winners." When an athlete is trained to look past personal glory, she begins to see that a champion's strength is measured by the virtues of the heart: the challenge is within, the opponent is one's self, and the reward is deeply personal and private. Through athletics, one can create a new level of awareness beyond sport.

When athletes focus only on prospects of winning, losing, points scored, and other results-oriented possibilities, they build up anxiety and tension because they have no control over these outcomes. When the thoughts shift to things they can control—their desire, commitment, persistence, courage, and confidence—they perform at their best more consistently.

When athletes gain inner strength they also experience something more in their sport and athletic participation, something that enables them to sustain more enthusiasm, excitement, and joy in their efforts. With the elements of inner strength, athletes are better able to experience the important alignment of body, mind, and spirit, a state that the Japanese refer to as *satori*—the perfect state or "zone" for the best performance. Six-time Hawaiian Ironman champion Mark Allen, perhaps the toughest triathlete ever, approached his sport by focusing on how his performance nourished his inner strength: "The race is just you against yourself . . . a very pure, enriching experience." He felt that every race taught him something about himself on a deeper level.

American cyclist Lance Armstrong has changed his relationship with his sport by developing his inner strength. He says he used to take his talents for granted and was a bit consumed by the glory, prizes, and material gain that came with being a professional cyclist. But after being diagnosed with cancer that had spread to his lungs and brain, he realized a strength and fight that he never knew he had. He survived his cancer with the help of aggressive treatments and took his newfound courage, persistence, and tolerance for pain and fear with him on the bike. When it came time for his first post-cancer Tour de France, he was well prepared to take it on. His eventual victory was a triumph on many levels—physical, emotional, and spiritual.

We wouldn't wish for any of our athletes to go through such an experience as Lance had in order to gain more perspective on their hard work or to tap into their inner strength. Athletes can, however, learn from stories of people who have discovered their inner strength, especially through sport. Coaches can use the strategies outlined in this chapter to instill in athletes a commitment, courage, confidence, and belief in themselves. These qualities will guide them to persist in striving toward their goals and maintaining their desire in an environment of selfless cooperation.

Athletes are perfectly capable of grasping all they need to become internally strong. They can do so if you are willing to help them to challenge how they see things and to shift their attitudes toward their performance and away from obsessing about scores and outcomes. In this way you can test athletes' limits and discover how they can achieve more satisfying levels of participation.

Commitment

Athletes who display deep desire and discipline have a strong commitment to succeed. *Commitment* makes an athlete put that desire into action by setting aside the time, effort, and patience to be the best she can be. It is what distinguishes great athletes from good ones. When one is committed, the sky's the limit.

But commitment doesn't have a life of its own. It will begin to fade if it's not nurtured and fed. Your plans, objectives, and goals can motivate your athletes to persevere until results are achieved. These goals must be attainable, or frustration and disappointment will quickly set in. They must also be challenging, or boredom and burnout will result.

To measure an athlete's level of commitment, ask, "What four things are you willing to do in practice each day [or in each competition] to prove to yourself that you are serious about your commitment to the team, the coach, and your own personal improvement in this sport?" I have heard answers such as "give verbal support to teammates," "help the coaches with equipment care, distribution, and collection after practice," "sprint on defense to go for the 50/50 ball," and "work out five days a week in the off season." Once these answers are specified, the athlete can write affirmations from them on index cards (see "Use Affirmations," page 151). I ask the athletes to share their "big four" with their teammates, which makes them more accountable to everyone. These smaller commitments can be upgraded or replaced weekly as an athlete begins to approach the bigger goals, the greater overall picture.

To further demonstrate their intent, have athletes create a contract and sign it as an outward expression of their commitment. Copies can be made and distributed to other teammates, and coaches can keep a copy on file. Draw up a contract for individual athletes that centers on a team objective or plan. I have used the contract on the following page with teams and coaches very successfully.

This exercise creates the opportunity for athletes to be responsible and accountable for their commitments. Monitor the athletes' responses to be sure they are challenging, expansive, and aligned with your mission for the team. By having frequent (weekly or every other week) team meetings on the subject, you can talk with individual athletes, give them feedback, and work with them to adjust their choices.

I, _____ [print name], pledge with all my heart to participate on the _____ [team name] team in practice and games as if I am a significant contributor [or "national-class champion," or other appropriate phrase]. To show how serious I am, I commit to

1. _____

2. _____

3. _____

4. _____

I accept my role on this team and will fulfill it.

SIGNED _____

Have athletes write down specific tasks that will enhance their commitment.

Be sure to not use this meeting as a punitive checkup session; there is no need to blame, condemn, or criticize. This is simply an opportunity to teach and to guide and support their choices. Listen to athletes' observations and comments about their progress. Invite them to change or revise their big four, especially after they've had the chance to view their teammates' commitments. When an athlete seems to be down or performing poorly, remind her to think about the contract and what can be done to get back on track. You might ask, "Beth, what is standing in your way of doing those four things you committed to doing? Is there some way I can help? Are there new actions or approaches that would help turn things around for you?"

Athletes who are truly committed are willing to see setbacks and failures as learning opportunities. Low-commitment athletes, on the other hand, often see their setbacks as justification to abandon their dreams. When there is deep commitment, there is little room for excuses for marginal performance. Discouragement and disappointment are recognized as natural and are tolerated. Committed athletes have an undying thirst for new, innovative ways to improve and are willing to put forth extra effort when needed.

Seek creative ways to encourage and inspire athletes with their own commitments. Try having the athletes post their commitments on their lockers, or have an athlete talk about a particular commitment and what it personally means to him. Create the opportunity in your next meeting for athletes to determine what they think is best for them, rather than the coaching staff choosing for them. When athletes do this, they increase their chances for success because they feel a greater personal investment. Ask athletes to write their commitments on index cards and recite them daily to help reinforce their directions. For example,

I, _____ [name], am strongly committed to _____. When I _____ [write in commitment], I demonstrate my seriousness as a highly committed athlete.

Encourage athletes to visualize these commitments as if they were actually happening.

Remind your athletes to keep commitments realistic and positive. For example, they should avoid saying, "I commit to not making turnovers"; better to say, "I play heads-up and remain alert. If I falter, I learn and correct the mistake." Instead of saying, "I commit to never being negative," the athlete could say, "I look for ways to be positive to my teammates during each practice and game."

As we discussed in chapter 4, establishing clear roles on the team for athletes helps raise their sense of commitment by demonstrating that their contribution to the team has an impact and provides a specific purpose. The athletes' satisfaction in knowing that they truly "count" and play a significant role in the team's mission keeps their commitment alive.

Without true commitment, an athlete's level of performance will consistently fall short of her abilities. High levels of performance are only possible when one dedicates oneself to a specific, worthy cause wholeheartedly.

Make sure that an athlete's role and contribution have meaning and that they make a difference.

Persistence

In the 1984 Olympics in Los Angeles, world-class swimmer Pablo Morales missed the gold medal in the 100-meter butterfly by an arm's length. Four years later he set a world record but failed to make the Olympic team. He persevered with his training and his desire for the gold for four more years, and in 1992 at Barcelona he won the gold in the 100-meter butterfly. The world of sport is filled with teams and individuals who have the desire to win, are committed to the journey, and persist through many setbacks and obstacles to achieve a lifelong dream.

Persistence is a deliberate mind-set and "heart-set" that keeps an athlete moving toward the attainment of a vision, particularly during discouraging times. Athletes who persist determine in their minds and hearts that once they commit, they must continue striving until the task is completed. They are convinced that even though they may fail a hundred times, if they persevere they will succeed by either obtaining their goal or being enriched in the experience of trying. Desire, commitment, and persistence are crucial pieces of the puzzle for athletic success—particularly for the internal success of athletics, which often means more than external championships, even though the championship or outcome is part of the goal. While it's possible that an athlete may not reach his ultimate goal having these crucial three elements, he certainly won't reach his goal *without* these components of success.

Being persistent requires a sense of trust in the process, knowing that with diligent effort over time, you advance and often achieve your goals. Without trust that positive results will occur if you put the time in, persistence is difficult to maintain. To creatively help athletes to persevere, reinforce any positive movement they make in the right direction. Say, "I know you can do it; just keep it up, you're on target." Remind them that many athletes became discouraged and almost gave up just prior to their biggest breakthroughs. Maurice Green almost gave up track completely before the 1996 Olympics. He watched the 100 meters in 1996 from the stands and vowed that as long as he was running, he would never miss a 100-meter final again. Having made this promise, he sought out a new coach to achieve his goals. He found that coach in John Smith. Three years later Green set the world record in the 100-meter run, and four years later he won the gold medal in the 2000 Olympics.

During my competitive running days, I finished second or third in many big races, seemingly unable to get the win. I began to get discouraged, and after three years I thought I was through. A national-class running coach encouraged me to keep up the hard work and to persevere. He said that if I did, my day would come. He suggested I use a few competitive strategies, such as surging at crucial moments in a race, and see what they would bring to my racing. I tried the tactic at my very next race, a marathon, and registered my first victory for that distance. I then went on to win five of the next six races I entered. I am now able to push through discouraging times because I have learned that with hard work and clear focus, the palm trees usually appear on the horizon in due time.

This trust in the payoff of perseverance requires a certain level of maturity. You can cultivate athletes' willingness to persevere if you help them focus on the joy of the process and on appreciating the journey over the goal or destination. A way to do this is to ask the athletes about their early relationship with their sport: What did they love about it? Why did they continue to be involved? Answering these questions helps refocus them on the essence of why they identify themselves as athletes of their sport, and can help them to fan the fires of passion and remind them of the joy of the process.

Another way to help athletes to see the value of persistence is to discuss the benefits of plateaus in performance—both in training and in competition. Fearful of reaching a plateau in their training, athletes often become impatient and frustrated with what they

Persistence paid off for world-record holder Maurice Green. Coaches can help athletes break through discouragement and performance plateaus.

sense to be a lack of progress. It's important, however, that coaches help athletes to understand plateaus as essential holding patterns on the journey toward mastery. Plateaus are important periods of learning through repetition with variation, periods in which athletes can adapt and become familiar with a new level. We only go forward when the time is right, not when we think we should move ahead. Point out how the experience itself is of great value and is worthwhile; explain that a plateau represents a period of deeper understanding, development, and maturity. Trying to force through this time could result in injury, setback, and discouragement.

With all its twists and turns, its changes in direction and speed of flow along the way, the river eventually finds its way to the sea. This image is one of ease and hopeful anticipation. When athletes learn to see things in this way, they no longer confuse persistence or perseverance with suffering. To help them understand the concept, ask them to look back on a time when they were experiencing a plateau—playing well, perhaps, but without much improvement. Ask them what they feared at this moment, and whether that fear ever materialized. Usually, athletes realize that there is little reason to fear and that breakthroughs occur when you cast worry to the wind. Help them to relax and enjoy the process of improving. Plateaus are a natural part of progress.

Naturally, these same principles hold true even during a game or event. Sometimes athletes force things, trying to make something happen rather than simply continuing to do what works. Falling behind in any way demands that an athlete take on the storm and persist—keep coming at those things that seem to be standing between her and her goals. Things do turn around when one refocuses and applies intensity. It helps athletes when their coaches understand the function of plateaus and do not become impatient with players who are not improving as quickly as they think they should. By modeling this patience and by persevering along with the athletes, you teach them to accept the pace they are on.

*Plateaus are necessary stages of rest,
repetition, and learning on the road
to new levels of performance.*

Persistence is an important trait to have as an athlete, perhaps more important than talent. It has been said that talent accounts for a mere 5 percent of most achievements, and persistence and hard work fill out the rest. Even the most talented of teams and athletes fail; they can't control outcomes. But persistence and perseverance are qualities you can control and develop. It's up to you to commit to staying on track, to push through in the face of the harshest adversity. All champions, bar none, have developed this trait.

There is an expression I picked up while working with a professional mountain bike team: *All is possible—it's just time in the saddle.* Becoming good at any sport requires many hours of persistent, diligent work. Getting to the podium often requires two steps to the side, one step back, and one step forward. That's why we practice.

When athletes become disheartened with their performance, refocus them on their strengths. High levels of frustration may be the result of setting goals that are unreasonably high. Persistence may never help in such cases. For example, no matter how long I persist, I will probably never make it into the NBA as a point guard. That goal would be unreasonable in light of my obvious shortcomings. Persistence will pay dividends, but a coach needs to help athletes to understand that the way to set up goals is to take manageable steps on the way to sky's-the-limit goals. Some athletes may have more small steps to take along the way than others, but by breaking down the goals into manageable parts, most athletes can go as far as they desire. Remind them of the role compassion plays when setbacks occur (chapter 2, page 55). It's good to reevaluate goals and objectives with respect to where you are and where you possibly can go. As a coach, you know your athletes; help them stretch and persist in that direction. With patience and a relaxed mind-set, things come faster.

Help your athletes to develop their ability to persist by doing the following:

- Put the joy and fun back into the process of accomplishment. Find ways to reward athletes for small gains. For example, create a progress graph and hang it up in a place where others can see how much everyone is improving. Choose an athlete of the week based on specific criteria.
- Encourage athletes to find the courage to act and to take risks.

- Ask athletes to seek support from others when times are rough. Talking to peers who have had difficulties and reading about athletes who have struggled prior to breakthroughs are ways to gain support and to become inspired to persevere.
- Remind athletes that progress is usually made up of forward, backward, and lateral movement.

Courage

It is widely known within horse racing circles that when horses die, only champions receive a burial ceremony. And what they bury is the heart, the part of the anatomy that enabled the horse to never let up—to run all-out regardless of the pain. Champion athletes, like horses, compete with their hearts, having the courage to give it their all under most circumstances.

The University of Maryland women's field hockey team had just beaten Old Dominion University 3-2 in overtime, gaining a slot in the Final Four in Boston. My work with Maryland throughout the year consistently emphasized the need for the athletes to play with their hearts (courage) and the importance of the team over the individual. This is always a challenge with a team of many stars. Following their victory, the Maryland Terps received the highest of compliments and greatest validation for their efforts. The Old Dominion coach said, "Maryland competed, hustled, and played with their hearts. When a team does that, it is very difficult to beat. Maryland won as a team."

What did the coach mean by "They played with their hearts"? I would define *heart* as the willingness to take risks to improve, even in the face of potential failure; the courage to go all out and discover your capability at the moment; the freedom to lose, learn from it, and forge ahead; playing with fearlessness, tenacity, and audacity; being bold as you look at your opponents and dare them to match your intensity.

For champions, this is the spirit of play. Athletes playing only with their heads tend to be too ego involved, smitten with themselves, and overly concerned with outcomes and winning. Courageous athletes and coaches, on the other hand, have a deep desire to win—but if they don't win, they refuse to measure their self-worth by any outcome.

A coach helps a team cultivate courage by giving the athletes the freedom to fail. They all learn, therefore, that mistakes and setbacks are necessary components of the improvement process. Learning from these failures helps to develop the most challenging, difficult athletic skills. If you do not have the freedom to fail, you take no risks and come to a full stop on the road to greatness.

Create an environment in which athletes are free to fail.

When your athletes fail, suggest that they step back, embrace the failure, and learn from it; if necessary, guide them to change direction. All athletes should know that you see failure in this way and that courage is what you expect. Then, when failure of any kind occurs, take the time (immediately at practice, perhaps the next day if it occurs in a game) to ask the athlete, "What did you learn from that situation? What could you do to prevent such mistakes in the future?" Rather than fighting their failures, athletes gain from seeing them as a natural experience that must occur. When they feel most devastated from taking a risk and suffering a setback, they can be reassured that they are about to learn from the experience in some way that will help them improve. If they overlook this lesson or resist learning it, they will create new limitations that will impede their performance.

Specifically, ask your athletes to demonstrate courage by accepting embarrassment when it comes. This may mean diving for control of a loose ball or coming back after taking a hard shot to the head. It may mean holding their heads high when losing a game if they went all out. It may involve taking the open shot after having already missed five in a row, facing the crowd on the opponents' home court, and doing the right thing in all situations.

To help athletes harness their courage to take risks to improve, have them imagine the worst-case scenario of taking a particular risk. If they can accept the downside, encourage them to go for it. If not, they may need to wait until they're more prepared. I once asked my son, Sean, a 12-year-old point guard, what the worst thing would be if he took the risk and drove to the basket with someone tightly guarding him. He said he was afraid he'd get knocked to the floor by someone much bigger than him. "Maybe," I said, "but it's also possible that your defender will pick up a foul and your shot will go in, even if you get a little hurt." The very next game he decided to go for it and drove hard to the basket. He ended up scoring 12 points; he got pushed to the floor once but quickly recovered.

In all circumstances, an athlete should plan for risk-taking by thinking through the possible consequences; this is what Sean and I did. Then when the time comes to play, the athlete can go all out, no questions asked. If you fail to plan, you plan to fail. Planning increases the probability for success and lowers the risk factor and also enables you to *improve your planning* the next time from risks taken.

You know that most risks you've seen athletes take work out positively. Their fears about failure frequently don't materialize, and they often feel better having taken the risks. You can encourage athletes to take more risks by stopping play during practice when a risk is taken and saying, "That's good! I like it when you try something new. I love the way you took that chance." This way you recognize the risk-taking behavior without regard to the outcome.

Emphasize to each athlete one risk that you really want him to take in a competition. For example, perhaps you want your distance runner to surge between the 2K and 3K point of his 5K race or to charge up every hill. Reward the risk and discuss the effect it has on performance after the competition. I'm not suggesting crazy, haphazard risks; think in terms of careful risk-taking in which the outcome would not be devastating. It's one thing to go all-out for every minute of a hockey game, and quite another to calculate specific moments of such effort. The latter is certainly safer and more within your control. All risks of this nature require courage to execute properly.

*Reward athletes' efforts to
plan and take risks.*

Confidence

When athletes display courage in their efforts and take calculated risks to improve, they will inevitably experience failure, setbacks, and loss. It's part of the playing field and needs to be accepted as such. However, with repeated setbacks, discouragement can set in, causing an athlete to lose confidence. Coaches can prevent this downward spiral by finding creative ways to help athletes focus on their strengths, the tangibles and intangibles they bring to the team, and the possibilities that await them. The principal method to creatively instill confidence in athletes is to affirm and reinforce the positive.

Use Affirmations

All performance is the result of what an athlete sees or visualizes and what she says or hears. What an athlete says or hears others say about a performance can be packaged in an affirmation—a strong, positive, concise phrase that makes firm one's goals and directions. Affirmations are statements or expressions that keep you on track. They are words that give you permission to open up to possibilities by changing repetitive negative voices into positive reinforcements.

For example, prior to the start of their field hockey season, the Maryland women hung the following affirmation in their locker room: "We are the NCAA field hockey champs; get comfortable with it." With such self-direction, the Terps became willing to do anything worthwhile to make this dream come true. They soaked up these words every day for five months, and as they took to the practice field they were intent on playing like they were serious about their mission. Everything revolved around their goal. They went 24-1 and won their conference and the NCAA title. The words an athlete uses are often the seeds of future realities, capable of transforming life.

Many athletes have been using strong, concise phrases during competitions and practices for years. However, these words are often negative and create movement counter to the athlete's or team's desired direction. There's a big difference between beneficial affirmations and "affirmations" that focus on the negative.

Negative words create anxiety and self-doubt, which hinder performance. The key is to reverse these negative habits of the tongue and mind and to speak in words that nurture potential. Try this test with your athletes to illustrate the power of words. Have them recite out loud the following two phrases as if they were true:

1. I am a strong, vibrant, talented athlete, capable of performing at high levels of excellence.
2. I am a weak, worthless, wilted slob who is wasting away in sport.

Have the athletes notice the difference in how they feel: in the first case, they probably feel excited, confident, energized, strong, hopeful, and motivated. After reading the second "affirmation," their bodies may drop and they will likely feel down, sad, hopeless, and bleak. This is how positive and negative words influence their performance as well.

Some athletes use more subtle negative affirmations, such as the long jumper who says to herself, "I will not foul" instead of the more positive "I will hit the board right on and jump far." The former statement focuses on the negative—what the athlete will not do—whereas the latter affirmation focuses on what kind of jump the athlete is looking for.

Try this with your athletes in the weight room or while they are doing push-ups: have them repeat out loud, over and over (even though it sounds silly!), "I love getting stronger, I can do it; I love getting stronger, I can do it." Then have them do another set of the exercise, this time repeating over and over "I hate this workout, I can't do it; I hate this workout, I can't do it." Have the athletes compare their strength in each instance. How much stronger do they feel when they use the positive affirmation?

Athletes who say "I can" and act as if this were so perform at higher levels of excellence more consistently.

For the past 23 years I have trained professional, Olympic, collegiate, and high school teams and athletes in the proper use of affirmations as a performance tool. A big part of my work is to instill in each of these teams and athletes the empowering words

I can. When you affirm *I can,* you stimulate the central nervous system with excitement, confidence, and courage, all positive qualities that open this system to the unlimited boundaries of your performance potential.

As a creative coach, you can help your athletes in similar ways. Create both team and individual affirmations to be posted on the locker room walls and personal lockers as daily touchstones. I ask athletes to create a pack of index cards, with one affirmation per card, to carry along with them and to flip through them when time permits. Or they can place these cards in various places at home, such as in drawers or on dressers, so that they see them throughout the day.

Use the following guidelines to create your best affirmations.

- The phrase should be short, pithy, concise, and simple.
- It should be positive, affirming what you *want,* not what you don't want. Avoid statements such as "I will not crash today." Instead, say, "I ride with the skill of a champion."
- Use the present tense. Frame your statements as if the future were now. Rather than "I will finish in the top 10," say, "I finish in the top 10."
- Act as if your affirmation were true, and it will keep you on track.
- Be consistent. Recite affirmations for a few minutes each day, instead of once a week for an hour. A good time to do this is during your visualization session. Picture what the words say.
- Use rhythm. A cadence or rhyme will help you remember a phrase more easily, for example, "I'm in a position to *strike,* and win on the *bike.* "

Here are some examples that follow these guidelines:

Self-image affirmations

I love and appreciate myself.

Lean and trim, I perform to win.

I am a whole and complete athlete.

Ability

Every day in every way, I run faster and faster.

Calm and confident, I play [or run, or swim, or . . .] well.

Effortlessly, I glide like a tireless deer.

Opponents

Good competitors bring out the best in me.

My opponent is not important—I'm well trained.

I am in control and ready to roll.

Confidence

I improve with each move.

I perform in good form above the norm.

I may not win, but I'll run one incredible race.

Concentration

Focus now, focus now, focus now.

I keep my mind on the task at hand.

Distraction facilitates attention.

Goals

I control the goal and go for the gold.

Setbacks are opportunities that help me reach the goal.

Expect success.

Injuries

Healthier and stronger, longer and longer.

My limber, flexible self restores itself to health.

Health is me; I'm injury free.

When athletes use affirmations they should imagine the "pictures" created by the words; in a relaxed state, the central nervous system will process the words as if they are real and will help the athlete act and behave in ways that increase the probability of these images becoming reality.

Affirmations are self-directions, not self-deceptions.

Use Mistakes as Learning Opportunities

There are other creative ways to help your athletes gain confidence. When athletes are emotionally distraught, chastising them or drawing attention to their inadequacies can only complicate an already dismal confidence situation. A more positive approach is to help the athletes understand what might have gone wrong. Ask them what they think could be done in similar future situations to correct the problem.

As discussed in chapter 9, mistakes are our best teachers. Point out to athletes that they will experience a surge of confidence when they focus on the corrected behavior and know that they can create the necessary changes to become even better. In this way, you can help players regain confidence in their ability to go beyond the setback and to become better athletes in the process. You will also increase athletes' confidence in your coaching ability and enable them to be more relaxed and effective in turning things around. Knowing that you accept mistakes as natural steps on the path to success, athletes won't be afraid to take risks again to improve.

What about athletes who lose confidence prior to competition, even though they haven't experienced setbacks in the recent past? I talk frequently with players who have lost their confidence and ask, "How can I get it back?" I find that 95 percent of the confidence that they are referring to is related to what we truly cannot have—confidence over outcomes, aspects of sport that we cannot control. If we could, there would be no contest. There's a great expression that sheds light on this: *When the archer shoots for the love of shooting, she has all the skill; shooting for the gold, she goes blind.* When an athlete focuses on the moment, the joy of the event, he has all the confidence; when he focuses on outcome, he loses it.

Focus on the Process

Athletes can restore their confidence by concerning themselves with what can be controlled. Several coaches I work with have had success guiding their athletes toward what is possible for them at their level. These coaches employ a method called *process focus* that consistently gets results. Say you have athletes who obsess about beating their opponents, going for the title, controlling others; they naturally become anxious, stressed, and tense, and build layers of self-doubt because they can't control these outcomes. As a result, their performance suffers.

To reverse the traditional tendency of focusing on results, ask your athletes, "How do you need to be in order to be your best?" This question helps athletes to focus only on those aspects of performance they can control such as their preparedness, boldness, courage, and enthusiasm. As a result of being able to control these elements of performance, the athletes become relaxed, fluid, and empowered, and regain confidence in the process of playing at their own level of ability. The coaches and athletes sit down together and discuss this new focus. The athletes create such affirmations as, "I am a courageous athlete, capable of playing my best at any given time," or " I am ready to demonstrate what I can do each minute of play."

I remind athletes that opponents will always look in their eyes prior to a game. What they see often determines the outcome, because they will react to seeing your confidence, fearlessness, and courage. I say, "Let them see the fire in your hearts, your courage—and dare them to match your intensity." Again, this is a focus that's more manageable for an individual. Most athletes know that they can demonstrate courage and intensity when necessary. Ask an athlete to show you intensity during practice for 10 minutes. It's often as simple as that. Again, note how this reinforces performing with a focus on what one can control as opposed to the mind-set of "crushing" an opponent.

Train athletes to have confidence in
how they play the game.
The process, unlike outcomes,
can be controlled.

There are moments when athletes may *feel strongly* that they are going to win, and that's good. However, to expect nothing less than victory will produce excessive anxiety. Better to focus on the process of how you will be and how you'll compete during the contest, to expect yourself to be courageous, fearless, intense, patient, and daring, and to let the outcome be the by-product of this approach. Coaches who handle competition expectations in this way have calmer athletes who perform with enthusiasm. The athletes obtain *power*—not necessarily the power to dominate an opponent, but the power to demonstrate their own abilities and get the best out of themselves. Confidence is not about whether you are a better team or athlete than your opponent; it's about who puts it all on the line, who has the courage to risk, to suffer, and to feel fear.

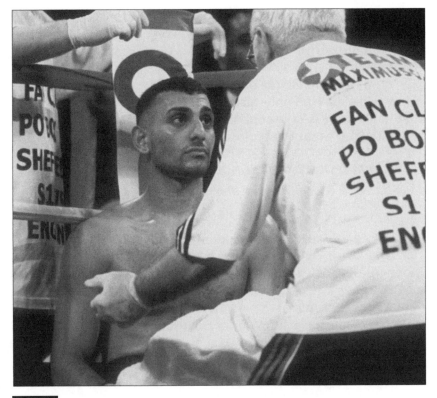

Naseem Hamed listens to his trainer. Athletes can control their own performance by controlling the courage, intensity, and confidence they bring to the match.

The Maryland women's lacrosse team was down 4-3 at the half to archrival Princeton. Coach Cindy Timchal chose not to try to "pump 'em up" for confidence. Cindy decided to remain calm and to instead focus her athletes on their commitment to being courageous and bold, and doing the specific things they could control like sprinting back on defense. She told them, "You know, you may or may not win. Just have confidence in knowing you can control how you play, like the NCAA champs you are. Play with integrity and demonstrate the four or five things you promised to do for this game. You are winners regardless of the outcome." With this peaceful message and the inner assurance that they could play with confidence, they went on to beat their nemesis by a score of 16-7. They "owned" the second half.

When the game concluded, little was said about the winning score; most of the talk centered on the internal triumph that all the athletes on the team were experiencing. They learned to tap into their "real" confidence by simply playing their own best game rather than fretting over catching and beating their opponent, things beyond their control. A team that gains overconfidence based on their results or outcomes experiences a false sense of security because no one can really be confident about something they can't control. True confidence is about knowing you can demonstrate your ability to perform.

Confidence is not about who is the best team or athlete. It's about who puts it all on the line, who has the courage to risk, to suffer, and to feel fear.

Building athletes' confidence is a process of diverting attention away from outcomes and toward developing a sense of the inner self, of focusing on the present and personal capabilities and readiness. Have athletes repeat each day the affirmation, "Calm and confident, I perform each moment like a true champion." This affirmation reinforces their confidence in their ability rather than in results.

Set the Stage for Success

Nothing builds confidence like success. Have your athletes develop short-term, realistic, attainable goals for daily practice and competition. For example, talk about the 10 things that they can do to perform better and measure their success by how they carry out these objectives. Each sport has small details that, when performed, result in big things happening. Working on a number of small objectives allows athletes to have more chances of receiving immediate positive feedback.

Diligently look for opportunities to set the stage for success. Gene Keady, Purdue men's basketball coach, helps instill confidence in his players by playing younger athletes at a time in a game when he believes they will be in a position to be successful. This builds their confidence. Keady believes that if you play young, inexperienced athletes in tough situations before they are ready, their confidence will take a beating, and they will begin to doubt whether they can contribute at the college level.

Past successes are wonderful confidence builders and reinforcers. Have athletes recall successful competitive performances from their past, noticing how they played and executed their moves with total confidence. Ask them to use these experiences as material to visualize how well they can play. This can be done in a group setting or in individual meetings with each athlete. Remind them that if they were capable of playing that well in the past, they can repeat or even improve upon that level of performance.

Belief in Limitlessness

Sometimes you may have a group of athletes whose self-doubt interferes with their being fully present and with doing what they can control and performing the "in-the-moment" tasks. They simply do not believe that they can control what they're meant to control. There is a breakdown in what should be true confidence. Perhaps the greatest advantage an opponent can have over you is your own lack of belief in your ability. Find ways to strengthen your athletes' *I can* power, their belief in their ability to control what they are capable of controlling.

Just thinking or saying *I can't* forces us to sabotage any efforts to discover the unlimited boundaries of our potential. When we shift our attitude to *I can,* we activate all the important psychological qualities—motivation, courage, commitment, excitement, joy, passion, enthusiasm—that steer us toward doing all we can to realize our performance dreams. Once Roger Bannister broke the long-standing belief in the four-minute barrier in the mile, the rest of the running world suddenly became motivated and excited about replicating his accomplishments. Within the next 18 months, over 40 athletes ran a mile in less than four minutes. Today, runners have proven that we can run two consecutive miles, each under four minutes.

All beliefs are limits; once we examine them, we can discover ways to go beyond them.

Don't think in terms of limitations; think instead of possibilities. Successful coaches encourage athletes to do things that seem impossible, and collect data that will encourage confidence and risk-taking. These coaches facilitate excellence in athletes by freeing them to explore possibilities. The athletes are able to examine their limited thoughts and beliefs about potential in an environment that encourages risk and tolerates failure; it is safe for these athletes to take on difficult challenges. In this way, the athletes discover ways to transcend their self-created obstacles.

One of my favorite coaches likes to say to his athletes, "It's inside you; I've seen it. I know you can do it." They all respond with a gleam in their eyes, excited about giving it a shot. He helps them focus on their strengths, what they do have, and reminds them that those strengths were once weaknesses that they probably didn't believe could be developed.

Increase the *I can* power of your athletes by encouraging them to read about others' success stories, those athletes who have beat the odds and ignored the limits placed on them by others or by circumstance. I like the story about the great Wayne Gretzky. When he heard someone say he was too small and too slow to play hockey, he refused to believe it. Most people told him he'd never play in the NHL, to which he'd respond, "That's a belief I'm going to change." Many elite Olympic and professional athletes like Gretzky have overcome limitations with the *I can* attitude, along with a lot of hard work.

Wilma Rudolph is another great example for any athlete who thinks, "I can't do that." She was one of 22 children born to a struggling family in rural America. As a child, she had polio and was told by her doctors that she'd probably never walk without a brace. In and out of hospitals for much of her early life, this ordinary person never lost her spirit; she believed that she could overcome this crippling disease. In miraculous fashion, at age 20, she became the first female to win three gold medals in an Olympics.

Like Wilma, most of us are ordinary people capable of extraordinary things; you simply need to believe you can and apply yourself accordingly. Ask an athlete to say *I can,* then encourage her to search for the truth and to collect the information that substantiates this statement. This mind-set enables the athlete to feel alive and to unlock the extraordinary potential that she inherently possesses.

In athletics, as in most of life, many of us decide before we even try what we can or can't do. Encourage athletes not to be rigid; when they feel themselves getting tight, ask that they keep a soft, flexible mind and believe with their heart that all is possible until the data comes back to prove otherwise.

Act as if all is possible until proven conclusively wrong.

Once I was hurting badly at mile 23 of a marathon. Rather than give up, I told myself *I can do this* and dug down deep to see what I had left. By claiming *I can,* I found hidden reserves and discovered how to work with my fear, fatigue, and self-doubt. This experience taught me to always challenge what I perceive to be limitations. I'm a better competitor because of this.

Constantly be on the lookout for your athletes' tendencies to think restrictively, and help them to discover ways to open up to greater possibility. Get them to refrain from self-criticism and encourage them to assume that all challenges are possible until something conclusively proves the contrary. Have them notice their limiting phrases and change them: "I'm not good enough" becomes "I have what it takes"; "I can't do it" becomes "I can"; "I don't deserve" changes to "I deserve"; "I'm not ready" changes to "I am right on schedule."

Use the following concepts to strengthen your athletes' confidence in performing well:

- Act as if. Have each athlete imagine another good athlete doing what he believes he can't do. Then ask your athlete to imitate that athlete in practice and during a competition.

- Use affirmations. Have athletes write phrases that establish the direction in which they wish to go. For example, a cyclist may believe that she can't climb hills. I would have her affirm, "I am a strong, powerful cyclist, capable of climbing with the best." Affirmations direct behavior toward the goal. By repeating these words when she climbs, she does those things that help her to climb better.

- Have athletes visualize situations in which their belief is an obstacle, such as if they feel they are too old, too short, too slow, or not good enough. Then ask them to see themselves performing as if they are able to perform with the skill they need. Athletes should reflect on the confidence they feel as they steadily progress and improve.

- Encourage athletes to challenge beliefs that block their way. When self-doubt creeps in and they feel they can't do something, have them ask, "How valid is my limiting belief?" Viewed within a larger context, their self-doubt will likely have little validity. Ask them to change the belief to its opposite and see how much more effective they become. For example, have an athlete change the statement, "I'm not good enough" to "I've got all that I need to be all that I want."

- Persistence is a virtue for accomplishment. When we persist, we notice higher levels of personal satisfaction.

- I invite athletes to embrace setbacks, learn from them, and make the appropriate corrections.

- In helping athletes to plan with their hearts, I help them to become courageous, risk-taking warrior athletes.

- My words create my reality, so I choose them wisely.

- I remind athletes of the tangible and intangible strengths they bring to the team.

- When I help my athletes to focus on how to be, their confidence increases and they feel victorious.

- When my athletes shoot for the moon and miss, they become one of the stars. They refuse to limit their potential by irrational beliefs.

Armed with their inner strength, commitment, courage, persistence, and confidence, and reinforced by affirmations, your athletes are now ready to focus on training their minds to strategize their performance. Mindfulness training is the subject of the next chapter.

part III

Unleashing Prepared Athletes

8

Strategizing With Focus

Demonstrate your greatness; don't try to dominate your opponent. Be ready, be prepared, and be the best you can be.

When most coaches think about strategizing, they immediately begin to think of Xs and Os—components of the physical and technical attack in competition. But there are other strategizing components that are important for optimizing athletic performance, those that guide the hearts, emotions, and minds of athletes. Although many coaches realize the importance of emotional and mental preparation, they rarely have specific strategies to use that will help their athletes in this regard. Other than a well-timed motivational talk, they leave to chance this most important component of performance. The creative ideas in this chapter will help you strengthen the "inner game" of your athletes by helping them to gain perspective on the essence of competition and to embrace attitudes and expectations that will keep them on the road to optimal performance. In a single year, coaches I have worked with used these strategies with seven teams who made it to a Final Four, two of them winning it all.

The mental focusing strategies presented here will help your athletes to be better prepared for practice and to carry out their game-day or competition strategy. Part of focusing effectively involves "living in the precious present." Never is that more essential than in competitions that are supposed to be easy, preceding a big game, match, or race. Those who look ahead—past the current contest and forward to next opponent—pay for it.

Athletes and teams who consistently perform at high levels play one game at a time. Coaches can encourage this through several measures. An old trick is to plaster the opposing team's or player's name on surfaces where players will see it often, like the locker room door or mirrors, to remind them of the task immediately before them. Another is to set specific targets for performance for each athlete for each game, making the successful completion of that mission a prerequisite to the next one.

With the right mind-set and "heart-set" athletes develop greater concentration and more confidence in their ability to execute the game plan. The concepts and tenets detailed in the previous chapters can help your athletes to better use this type of strategizing.

Absorb the Experience

Athletes need to be reminded to absorb their experience of participating in their sport—what they love about it and about the process of learning it and improving. Too many athletes get caught up in the media hype or the pressures of expectations and lose touch with the tremendous opportunity they've been given to participate in their sport. Losing sight of these aspects of their sport diminishes the overall experience. Many athletes' response to hype and expectation is anxiety, which reduces their chances for good performance. Athletes have earned the right to participate, and they compete at their best when they are into the moment, enjoying the process. I like to remind athletes that in this life, it doesn't get much better than the freedom to do what you love to do, and I encourage them to have fun and to enjoy the moment.

Most athletes have expectations about results that create anxiety and interfere with performance. You can foster a more positive experience by guiding athletes to focus on the process and their preparedness to take on anything—things they can control. For example, athletes can focus their expectations on the following:

Doing well

Making something really good happen

Demonstrating their present level of proficiency

Learning from experiences, successes, and setbacks

Being courageous

Staying positive and prepared

Sport is one of life's most rewarding pleasures, win or lose. Have your athletes consider not *whether* it's possible, but rather *how* it is possible. Ask athletes to dream things that never were and ask, *why not?* They can work together to come up with options that make their goals more possible.

Demonstrate, Don't Dominate

So many athletes and their coaches become sidetracked by strategizing their game or performance around how they can best dominate their opponent, a strategy no athlete can control. While athletes can't control an opponent, they do have the power to demonstrate their best plays, moves, and performance during the competition. Athletes can demonstrate (and facilitate) their own readiness for a competition or game. Competition is not necessarily about who's the best, the strongest, the biggest; it's about who has the biggest heart, the willingness to go all out and to dare others to match their intensity.

How can you get your athletes to play with more intensity? Start at one of your weekly or biweekly team meetings by asking athletes to describe what playing with intensity (or courage, or fearlessness, or tenacity) looks like in their sport. Then discuss how they can apply this same intensity by demonstrating that heartfelt quality for five minutes during that day's practice. Once they are able to achieve that intensity for five minutes, they have a reference point that not only shows them that they can do it, but also gives them a benchmark to try to beat in a competition for sustaining that intensity for longer and longer periods of time.

Athletes who focus on their own performance and work as a team are able to focus on playing with intensity during a competition.

The best way to help athletes with these qualities is to ask them what they can do athletically, skills-wise, decision-wise, to demonstrate courage, compassion, fearlessness, intensity, and other qualities. For example, athletes may say they demonstrate courage when they "surge up and over every hill" or "dive for every ball." Once they identify these specific actions, they can then commit to doing them. When they do, they play with courage and intensity.

In championship competitions, athletes think something special is going to be demanded of them beyond how they have been performing all season, but this is not true. Keep your athletes focused on their performance and why they are participating in their sport. Ask them, "What do you truly love about the sport? Why are you playing, really?" By staying in touch with the love and passion of play, athletes relax and attend to the "right stuff."

I recommend athletes do this with the coaching staff in an informal group meeting, as an exercise that strengthens team cohesiveness. For example, ask each person what he believes in most, what inspires him, and have each athlete place an image or reminder of his response on his locker. Some athletes may pick a passage from the Bible that moves them, or a poem, or lyrics from a song. Others may be inspired by a particular person, whether that person is related to their sport or not. When times get rough during the season, direct the athletes back to their own source of inspiration, to rely on it for strength. "Remember what you wrote about inspiration, in your locker?"

Here are some other questions athletes can ask themselves:

• *What is it like to compete against our team? How might our opponent feel?* Encourage your athletes to view the competition from the opponent's perspective. This will give them a refreshing view of their own team, who they are and how they play. A team might say, "We are relentless and tough—I'd hate to play us, because we never let up; we are always in their face; we are talented, strong, and very fast."

• *What message would we like to send to our opponent? What are we willing to do to show we are serious about this message?* These questions allow the athletes to consider the opponent but still focus on their own game, on what they are willing to accomplish—that which they can control. Some messages might include "We dare you to match our intensity," or "We will fall down in utter exhaustion or pain before we quit." Then athletes can consider specific ways to demonstrate their tenacity, courage, and fearlessness to their opponent: by sprinting on offense, diving for the ball, charging the net, and so on.

• *What four behaviors or traits will we demonstrate in practice or in the game this week to show how serious we are about raising our level of play?* Contemplating this question helps athletes to focus more specifically on the heart–mind strategies of their own performance. For example, they can choose to demonstrate more deliberate hustle, communicate with their teammates, keep their eyes on the ball, and dive for loose balls. Have each athlete choose four things he is willing to do and four ways he commits to doing them (see also chapter 7, page 140). Have them write their responses on index cards and sign them, like a contract. They can share this information with staff and teammates. By doing it in this way, they take responsibility, create accountability, and outwardly commit to staying in the moment, focused on what they can do rather than on results. When prepared athletes step into the competition arena, opponents will see passion, excitement, and intensity in their eyes.

• *What are the tangibles and intangibles I bring to the team?* An athlete may say, "I am fast, skilled, and experienced," for the tangible items, and "I am courageous, tenacious, and dependable" for intangibles.

• *What words would I like others to use in describing my style of play after I am gone? What am I doing today to make sure this happens?* An athlete may say that she wants to be remembered as a team player, a leader, a good communicator, a hard worker, and someone who played with integrity. After saying this, she must list concrete ways to show how she demonstrates these qualities.

• *How can I best serve the team?* This is a question that ties into what role an athlete plays on his team.

• *Why do I deserve to win today?* An athlete might answer this with, "Because I'm prepared, focused, excited, and ready to go all out, and I'm really good at what I do."

- *If I freed myself to play up to capacity, what would that be like?*

All meaningful journeys in athletics are guided by penetrating questions. Give athletes time during team meetings to contemplate their responses.

Have you noticed that when young children play, they don't worry about outcomes and results? They play for the love of playing, without expectation. The more childlike athletes can be, the more they play up to their capacity. When you see your athletes playing all out with heart, compliment them for such effort—that is how champions play. When they play this way, they will access "the zone" more often. Images of this kind of play are those that the athletes can and should use before practice and games during their visualization ritual. Athletes should also imagine themselves being and playing according to their answers to the questions presented in the preceding paragraphs.

Approach Competitors As Partners

In *The Ultimate Athlete,* George Leonard describes the true spirit of competition: "Every aikidoist [one who practices the martial art of aikido] faces the problem of finding a good partner who will attack with real intent. The greatest gift he can receive from his opponent is clean, true attack, the blow that, unless blocked or avoided, will strike home with real effect" (page 231).

The University of Maryland women's basketball team had just come off a frustrating 6-21 season. Coach Chris Weller and I talked about how their opponents served as partners along the road to higher performance, and acknowledged that when their opponents offered their best attacks and defenses, it could only help Maryland to raise the bar for themselves. Their mission the next season was to raise their level of play, to dig down deep and discover the courage, fearlessness, tenacity, and boldness necessary to perform at consistently higher levels every minute, every half, every game. They considered themselves successful when they committed to and achieved doing the little things such as sprinting up and down the court, boxing out, making assists, causing turnovers, and helping out on defense. Managers kept track of these details during each game. They were on a journey to find out just how good they could be. Naturally, the team would occasionally lose their momentum during the game or season, and at that time Chris would remind the athletes to reset and to refocus on those little things. Visualizing them on a daily basis really helped them improve.

All of this was in the spirit of competition. *Competition* comes from the Latin *competere,* which means "to seek together." With nothing to lose and everything to gain, the Terps played with their hearts, resulting in a winning season and a top 8 finish in the postseason WNIT tournament. Seeing their opponents as partners was indeed a new focus, one that was responsible for reinforcing the team's inner strength and confidence. By doing this, the athletes experienced a truer and more meaningful perspective on competition: Winning is important, but the best path to victory on the scoreboard is to focus on the process of participating and competing in a partnership with one another. This ultimately brings out the best in each athlete.

During the regular season, the Terps visited Duke and Virginia, beating these two powerhouses on their home courts using this new view of competition. Rather than being nervous about playing these top 10 teams, they embraced the opportunity to test how far they had come from the previous year and to demonstrate their level of excellence.

*Our competitors help us to play
up to our greatest potential.*

Successful coaches like Chris want to win, of course. Chris achieved this, however, by making mindfulness training a consistent team ritual and using the opposition to determine whether the preparation was working. They concentrated on seeing opponents in this more productive way and focused on what they could control—their style, effort, form, game plan, and preparation—to play more relaxed and with greater focus and intensity. In the true spirit of competition, we need to seek worthy opponents and be worthy opponents ourselves. By working together, we can achieve significant success.

The Chinese symbol for competition shows many individuals helping one another. All of your athletes' competitors serve to help them do their best, to push them to greater heights; and your team does the same for them. When athletes see competition in this way, they welcome the opportunity to take on an opponent in a more relaxed, focused fashion and they perform at higher levels on a more consistent basis. Creatively, you can help athletes see competition in a positive light by pointing out how all aspects of competition are a cooperative relationship among athletes, their teammates, and their opponents.

The more frequent and tougher the competition, the greater the opportunity to learn and grow.

Competition gives athletes the opportunity to learn the value of compassion for themselves and others when loss and failure occur. Competition is also about the relationship of the athlete to the team and the coach. Athletes have the opportunity to discover how working together as a team, pushing one another in training and competition, results in higher performance not only on the court but in all of life. You can witness what can be created by knowing that everyone truly wants the best for one another.

An athlete's relationship to the sport is also imperative. Sport is a great teacher, a microcosmic classroom of life. Athletics gives all of us the opportunity to find out what is real, what counts, what's important, all within a condensed period of time. Our society tends to teach us a one-dimensional view of competition, in which the opponent is the "bad guy," someone to be "beaten," "crushed," or "blown away." There is little athletic benefit to having such a view. Use the following exercise with your athletes to help them relate to athletic competition in a more expansive way and, as a result, to improve the overall quality of their performance.

Draw a one-inch line on a piece of blank paper. Ask your athletes what you can do to make it look smaller or less than it is. Many will erase some of it; others will fold the paper in half; some will move the paper into the distance. Note how these techniques do the job, yet cause you to focus too much energy on that line. Next, draw a five-inch line next to it and notice how the first line naturally looks smaller with respect to the new line. This is no different in competitive situations in sports and in life. When you enter the arena of competition, rather than focus on how to reduce the "enemy," concentrate on what you can do to make yourself better and use the opponent as a gauge to help you rise above it all. Athletes and teams can do this by using more effective tactics, improving specific skills, trying better equipment, practicing more effectively, and regarding the opponent as someone to treasure. All of these will "lengthen the line" of athletic growth and improvement.

Another good way to instill this view of competition in your athletes is to describe the playing field as a classroom. The athletes' opponents are *their* students and the athletes are the teachers. What lessons will your athletes teach their opponents? If you are preparing to compete against a particularly formidable opponent, remind your athletes that they may be the students today, but they can still try to teach these opponents some aspect of the game or sport. The day after the contest, ask athletes, "What did you teach the opponent? What did you learn?"

Both of these activities keep the perspective on competition as a way to seek together. The by-product of this is usually a good performance. To reinforce the partnership of competition, use the following visualization exercise.

Begin the ritual with meditation. Once a relaxed state is achieved, have everyone affirm this statement: "We are together today to help one another push the limitless boundaries of our potential." Imagine greeting your opponent in person through eye contact and mentally embracing him for being present. Feel fortunate and thankful that he agrees to bring out your best. Notice his pleasure in knowing that you both will do all that it takes to keep the other "honest." You both want to win. See the competitive event unfold. Feel the exhilaration of being challenged and rising to the occasion. The contest is now over. Thank your competitor and show appreciation by focusing on the level of play, not who won or lost.

When your athletes get into a tough situation—such as being behind in a competition—rather than trying to find a way to quit or get back at the opponent, they should simply ask the basic questions *What can I do now?* and *How can I use my opponent to help me?* When a runner floats by me at mile 20 of a marathon, rather than give up or try to catch him, I may decide to use this athlete, to let him pull me for the next half mile and then reevaluate the situation. By doing this I relax, benefit from my "partner's" energy, and may even discover reservoirs of strength I had not known I had. I dig deep because of my worthy opponent.

Help One Another

Athletes can strengthen their inner game by helping their teammates become greater. This is where the importance of challenging one another in practice comes in: team members should compete against one another with toughness and positivity. Have all athletes accept a leadership role on the team, rather than relying on one or two to do the job. Designated captains, chosen for the season or on a weekly rotational basis by the entire team and staff, should take care of details like the coin flip in a game and act as team representatives in talking with referees or calling for a team meeting when needed.

Don't let the team be fooled, however, into thinking that designated captains are the only true leaders. The common ground for most national championship teams that I work with is that leadership is everyone's role in getting involved with the team; encouraging others; setting good examples; and showing respect, courtesy, and loyalty. Athletes lead by serving their teammates during practice—always working in a way that helps their teammates improve. If athletes are not doing this, they are not being leaders and they are hurting their team. Ask athletes to earn respect as leaders by becoming aware of the various ways to demonstrate leadership and help their team.

Encourage your athletes to ask one another for help. More established players should take it on themselves to instruct the newcomers on skills and ways to improve. Pair up experienced athletes with the newcomers and encourage the older team members to act as mentors, taking younger players under their wings and helping them to learn the system, skills, drills, and so forth.

The athletes need to know from you that it's not the standings that are important—it's how they stand together over many rough miles of competition, win or lose, happy or sad. Have them verbally share their appreciation for one another in a circle during a meeting called for that purpose. How athletes express themselves to one another in this meeting is how they will express themselves in a game. Remind athletes to pursue victory in the context of cooperation, friendship, support, mutual respect, and compassion. This is total truth, learned through sports. It is also a good life strategy.

Open Your Mind

You are clearly the expert, the go-to person for your athletes, administrators, and other staff. Many experts assume they know it all or are afraid to admit they don't know something. But as an expert in your field, you should instead remain open to new information, options, and possibilities if you are to realize your full potential. In his bestseller *Zen Mind, Beginner's Mind,* Shunryu Suzuki states the following: "In the beginner's mind there are many possibilities; in the expert's mind there are few" (page 17). Sometimes there is an advantage to clearing our minds and focusing our attention on all the possibilities. Our preconceived biases and beliefs can prevent us from being more attuned to our surroundings. We are very busy with a myriad of projects, concerns, and issues at work and in daily life. As a result, it's difficult to focus on all the possibilities, and we become less effective in handling our tasks.

For these reasons, we all can benefit from a "beginners mind," a mind that is open, receptive, and nonjudgmental, a quiet mind to help us focus more clearly on the task at hand. Both coaches and athletes benefit from the practice of *mindfulness,* blocking out everything except that which they need to stay focused on in a specific moment.

Mindfulness is a focusing technique that helps one to zero in on the important details of the task at hand, be it practice or competition. In *Sacred Hoops,* Phil Jackson writes about how he used mindfulness techniques with the Chicago Bulls to bridge the team's vision (mission and goals) and the everyday, mundane reality on the court. This helped them to keep their vision alive when so much around them would distract and take them off course.

The players and staff were taught the skills of meditation and visualization to help their minds focus on those tasks that contribute in a positive way to the vision. For example, they could feel themselves executing specific offenses and defenses. Of course, some of the players rolled their eyes at the thought of this unusual method and didn't buy into its purpose. There really is no reason to force these techniques on your athletes. In the case of the Bulls, those who remained open gained quite a bit from the exercise. Meditation and visualization, when used consistently, will help athletes to accelerate their learning process, be better focused, strengthen confidence, and increase the chances of playing at higher levels on a more consistent basis.

You may experience resistance to this procedure from athletes when you first use it. I encourage you to add it to your daily rou-

The success of teams under coach Phil Jackson should inspire coaches and athletes to be open to the many benefits of mindfulness.

tine for a week or two and observe the results. You will notice that the athletes will practice and play more deliberately. You will all experience benefits in daily life outside the arena of athletics. Your team will be more relaxed, more productive, and more focused in all that they do. It takes time to train the mind. Like a muscle, the mind needs to be stretched and exercised daily if you want to develop it and make it strong. Coaches and teams find that this routine becomes a comfortable companion on the road to optimal performance. The benefits are numerous, including the opportunity for team members to be together, in a circle, quiet and reflective.

While athletes on your team may not buy into opening their minds up to all possibilities, you can help them see the importance of this training and accept the process by showing its relevance to the specific demands of your sport. Show them how this kind of mental practice can help them act with a clear mind and be present now, free of thinking, judgment, and extraneous "noise." It will also accelerate the process of learning any new skill. Mindfulness frees us from mental and emotional obstacles and allows us to focus on the present.

Mindfulness is a quick method to get focused, be in the moment, and become relaxed for optimal performance on a consistent basis.

Push Aside Mind Chatter

As you explore the value of mindfulness, it's important to find tactics for your athletes to effectively deal with the negative thoughts, fatigue, and pain that they will invariably experience, factors that create self-doubt, fear, anxiety, and stress before a big competition. They may not admit such feelings to you, but you can assume that they experience them. Conduct a team meeting and remind your players that even the best of the best have self-doubt and fear. Almost all the national and world champions, Olympians, and NCAA All-Americans I have worked with have fought against such mental obstacles. Our remedy has essentially been the same with each of these athletes—consistent daily meditation and visualization. Now, when these negative thoughts and feelings occur before or during a competitive event, these athletes say to themselves, *Look, I'm busy and need to get the job done . . . . I've got no time for you now. When the competition is over, I'll give you attention.* By acknowledging this negative talk, the athletes accept that it is there and thereby defuse the power it has over them. Trying to force the thoughts away or pretending they don't exist only makes the thoughts stronger. The energy you exert doing this complicates the existing problem. This technique works well with fatigue and other discouraging practice and competitive situations as well.

Meditation

Numerous coaches I've worked with have told me how meditation has helped them to broaden their awareness, be more creative, see more options, be more open to their own and their athletes' greatness, and be better able to detach from the "garbage" that clutters the mind. They say they enjoy their work at a much deeper, more meaningful level. The more they practice mindfulness in their daily lives as coaches, the more vital and effective they feel as leaders.

A well-respected coach at the University of Iowa told me that after the first session of mindfulness training, she and her athletes experienced one of the most productive practices ever; they showed up ready to go, on fire, willing to play all out. They were totally "there." The coaching staff felt a strong impact, coaching that day with greater zest and enthusiasm.

There are many techniques you can use to meditate or clear your mind. I use the following *breath watching* technique with the programs and teams I work with. This technique is appropriate for coaches to do on their own and with their athletes. Take 8 to 10 minutes to perform this daily mindfulness exercise approximately 20 minutes before practice and an hour before a competition. This gives you time to make the transition from the locker room to the playing arena.

1. Sit comfortably in a chair, keeping your back naturally upright and placing your feet in front of you, with your legs open naturally from your hips.
2. Close your eyes to reduce external stimulation.
3. Inhale very slowly through your nostrils and, with closed eyes, "watch" a white cloud of air enter and fill the lungs completely.
4. When lungs are full, hold the breath for five seconds and visualize the clean air traveling to all parts of your body

down to your toes. Imagine this breath picking up your tension and toxins.

5. Slowly release the air through your nostrils and notice the natural relaxation that occurs when the now-gray cloud filled with toxins, stress, and negativity exits as carbon dioxide. "See" this smoky cloud dissolve into thin air and disappear.

6. After a complete exhalation, once again suspend breathing for a second or two and imagine the wide-open emptiness of your lungs before you resume inhalation.

7. Repeat this process seven times or more. Gradually, feel your breathing spreading and penetrating outward into your arms and legs until the breath reaches the tips of your fingers and toes.

In this state of mind, you will feel very relaxed and "mind quiet." At this point, you can begin to focus on the visualization and affirmation aspects of mindfulness.

Visualization

Use vivid, positive images of yourself practicing and competing. Imagine simply playing your best, the way you know you can play. Try to include as many senses as possible as you visualize your perfect performance. Feel the exhilaration; feel the grip on your tennis racket; smell the air, the grass, the sweat; hear the crowd and your teammates. See the entire scope of the competitive event. Be the way you'd like to be as you play and do those things that show how good you can be.

Affirmation

Finish the mindfulness process by using an affirmation, a strong statement of direction that makes your intention positive and firm (see chapter 7, pages 153-155). For example, you may repeat, "Regardless of outcomes and results, I play like a champion," or "I am an incredibly strong, vibrant athlete and I give it my best at all times." As you recite the words, visualize them as if they are true. *Say, then see* is the key.

   The Duke University women's basketball team has used this technique with great success. In our first year working together, the team reached the Final Four using mindfulness training. Head coach Gail Goestenkors took 10 minutes with the team each day before practice; when she dimmed the lights in the locker rooms, everyone took that as the cue to clear their minds using the breath watching technique. With empty minds they began visualizing the upcoming practice or game, focusing on the task or plan and imagining themselves performing their best. Such a ritual enabled them to focus deeply on their short- and long-range goals. For example, not only would they visualize the goals of that practice session— they also envisioned playing in the Final Four, which increased their motivation, excitement, and commitment before practice. The coaching staff agreed that these mindfulness training techniques were crucial in raising the levels of play for all athletes. They experienced a stronger bond and team cohesiveness than they had experienced before.

Regular mindfulness training helped coach Gail Goestenkors and her Duke University women's basketball team realize their goals.

There are other techniques that can create an empty mind, relaxed and ready for visualization. Some teams use Hatha Yoga, a gentle stretching and breathing method that can produce similar results. Other teams place an object, such as a lit candle, in the center of their circle. They then concentrate on this object (in this case, the candle's flame) by focusing on it, clearing their minds of all else, which helps them to relax and focus.

The success teams have had with the breath watching technique suggests that it's worth the time and effort. It includes all the necessary ingredients in the preparation of one's body, mind, and spirit—mind-clearing meditation, visualization, and words that positively affirm your objective. When an athlete shows up to practice or play, regardless of age or experience, distraction is the norm. School work, social life, family dynamics, fear, self-doubt, anxiety, fatigue—all interfere with the ability to be ready, focused, and in the moment. Thus the need for creating an empty mind. A clear mind is like a sponge, which, when exposed to appropriate images, soaks them up as if they were real. Relaxed, calm, energized, and focused, the athletes and coaches become ready to be present for the task.

Mindfulness gives you more confidence to do what you can control and to let go of what you can't.

Don't confuse this particular mindfulness training with other "soft" exercises in relaxation. Once your mind has been cleared and your body relaxed, mindfulness is the process of focusing on specific aspects of your game. It is a solid, practical way to "park your attention" in what has become known as *the zone*. Mindfulness helps you to tune in to the subtle details of the game by blocking out all external distractions. It is a way to restore true confidence by focusing on specific aspects of play that you can control.

For example, remember the four specific things that your athletes pinpointed as things they could do to raise their level of performance? Once the athletes can identify these behaviors, they can then place them on index cards as affirmations to be repeated each day and to serve as reminders of how to stay focused throughout the event. In the visualization segment of mindfulness training, have an athlete imagine playing and demonstrating these qualities as if they were really doing so.

It is crucial to keep a consistent daily ritual or routine with mindfulness if you are to experience its full benefit. Some of you are probably thinking that you simply do not need one more thing to do in your day. However, the time you spend alone or with your team clearing the mind, focusing, and visualizing will enable you to have more effective practices in less time, thus also helping with the potential problem of excessive training (see chapter 6). Several coaches have told me that a 10-minute ritual of mindfulness enables them to accomplish their regular practice session 30 minutes sooner, an overall savings of 20 minutes each day! When you take the time to practice mindfulness training, you show up more focused, more present, ready to work, and you can usually perform at higher levels in less time. After all, when you have one eye on practice or a game and one eye on something else, they invariably cross and prevent you from attending to what's going on now, prolonging the learning curve. Take 8 to 10 minutes and include mindfulness in the total workout time. Perform the ritual 10 minutes before practice or working out (weights, cardiovascular training) and either individually on the morning of a competition or an hour before the competition as a group.

Over the last 10 years, 23 of my teams who have used this mindfulness training have gone on to the Final Four; 12 have won national championships. Twenty-one of my individual athletes have won national titles using this approach over the same 10-year span. Mindfulness definitely facilitates your chances to perform at your best.

- I get my athletes to strategize with their hearts and minds. When we do this, I am able to unleash thoroughly prepared athletes.

- When I help my athletes to see their competitors as helpful partners, they relax and live up to their potential, free of anxiety and tension.

"Seeking together" in sports is an art, one that takes time to cultivate. When you focus on this "new" way, working together will help you to achieve heights you never dreamed possible as your former enemy becomes your teacher and vice versa. With this approach, your athletes will be able to waltz into any arena of play with a sense of relaxed intensity, prepared to experience being the best they can be.

9

Succeeding Through Victory and Defeat

Winning is often the result of attending to the process instead of the product.

Are you wondering how *winning* and *losing* can be presented together as two ways toward achieving success? I purposefully present both winning and losing here, because losing is such a necessary component of ultimately winning. We only win when we are able to handle loss. We need to tolerate and accept failure. When we do, we relax, learn, and forge ahead. This is truly the success of defeat.

Someone recently told me that my three-page resume was quite impressive. I acknowledged the compliment but added that he had not seen the equally "impressive" three hundred pages of setbacks and failures, without which those other three pages would not even exist. Like any accomplished person, I acknowledge that my achievements are the by-products of my failures. These failures have taught me through trial and error how to continue to improve and to eventually get it right. Loss—if you open yourself to learning from it—is gain. In order for this to happen, you must actively embrace failure and use it as a tool for eventual success. All significant gain is necessarily preceded by loss.

Learning From Loss

Some of the really great coaches of our time did not begin their careers with the winning records we see attached to their names now. Coach Krzyzewski's first three years at Duke were rather tentative. In the highly competitive, powerful Atlantic Coast Conference, his teams were 13-29 over those beginning years. Coach K understood that we learn from our losses, that great things come from adversity, and he chose to use these beliefs as tools to help his team stick it out, learn, and eventually forge ahead. You, too, can adopt this mind-set. Many notable coaches have used their failures as building blocks for future success.

Losses, setbacks, and failure are natural,
valuable teachers on the path to success.

When the second-ranked University of Kentucky men's basketball team was shaken by an unexpected home court loss to South Carolina, Kentucky coach Rick Pitino wasn't. He understood that this was an opportunity to learn and to become a better team. He took all he could learn from the slaughter and focused his team on the loss as a lesson in attitude. They had been overconfident, had played without intensity, and had failed to live up to their commitments. He embraced the loss as a teacher, instructing his players about their shortcomings and the changes they needed to make to overcome them. From that point on, they breezed through the NCAA tournament, making it to the finals for the second consecutive year only to lose a close, disappointing match to the University of Arizona. Although they learned some things that would help them in later seasons and all of life, this was a tough loss for the Kentucky Wildcats and they needed time to recover before the finer lessons could be learned. After a while, they began to get a clearer perspective, one that enabled them to see what they needed to learn to get to the next level.

Great coaches and elite athletes experience many setbacks in their careers, but because they understand that failure is our best teacher, they listen closely to this wisdom and are able to proceed. Michael Jordan was cut from his high school team as a sophomore, but thanks to a supportive teacher—his dad—Michael learned to fight back and get stronger. (It didn't hurt that he grew six inches between his sophomore and junior seasons.)

The sport of basketball, and the world, would be considerably poorer had Michael Jordon given up when faced with failure.

The records are filled with athletes who understand the principle that we win by losing. Creative coaches can help themselves and their athletes to better grasp this principle by going back over past failures of their athletes and helping them realize how valuable the experiences were. It is also helpful to discuss games after they are played (the next day), to watch videotapes of the performance and ask, "What can we learn here?" Have your athletes keep a journal or fill out a postcompetition questionnaire as part of their routine, then discuss their thoughts in a one-on-one or team meeting. Help them see that most of what they know and what they can do is the result of having had failure or setbacks. This is how we all learn and improve.

Tolerating Loss

Buddhist thought has been credited with the observation that the arrow that hits the bull's-eye is the result of a hundred misses. In archery, it is the champion marksman who has the most failure, and the elite athlete who makes the most mistakes. The main difference between the great athletes and the almost great is that the great ones have cultivated, over a period of years, a high tolerance for mistakes, setbacks, and failures. They may not have welcomed the failures, but they allowed for them as a necessary part of their learning and improving. They know the inevitability of such errors and their role as a teacher. They take lots of shots at the target, correct their aim as they go, and never let the misses become the excuse to quit. Most who never "make it" give up just before the palm trees appear on the horizon. Winners see loss as a gift, and success comes to them because they can tolerate, and then become better able to see their way out of, the storm. For winners, losing is valuable data, helping them to understand the big picture of championship levels of play.

*Winners are those who have experienced
the most mistakes.*

Creative coaches help themselves and their athletes to get beyond the traditional notion of failure as an abomination to be avoided at all costs. They encourage the risk-taking that is necessary to reach full potential. They help their athletes embrace adversity, using it in a positive way to rebound from setbacks. Athletes learn through you, the coach, tolerance and acceptance of loss as well as how to turn defeat into eventual victory and crisis into the opportunity to improve.

To help your athletes better tolerate losing, try the following thoughts used by several of the successful coaches I work with, explaining to your players the reasoning behind these thoughts.

- All physical skills, no matter how difficult, are always perfected through mistakes and failures. Think of the way children learn to walk (the most difficult physical skill to learn) or how to ride a bike: by falling and getting up again and again.
- All great athletes identify what they have learned in defeat and begin to see how it helps them to higher levels. Recall with your athletes some stories of great athletes and teams who experienced big loss, learned in defeat, and used it to their advantage.
- Notice how it is absolutely impossible for any athlete to always be successful, competent, and highly accomplished in sports, or any arena of life. Ups and downs are natural; you win some, you lose some.
- Refuse to fight with yourself when failure and loss pay an unexpected visit. It is healthy to take ourselves less seriously.
- Failure is not devastating. Disappointing, yes! If athletes give it their all and lose or fail, tell them that you'll still love them and want them on your team.
- Failure is part of the process of successful living. Real failure, perhaps the only failure, is your unwillingness to understand the role of setback in creating success.
- You can't avoid failure. There are only two kinds of athletes: those who fail, and those who will. So begin to see its value.

You can assist your athletes' progress by using a more creative approach to failure: create an environment that encourages them to take risks to improve. In that environment there is the freedom to fail—and success is not possible without this freedom. Then offer them compassion (see chapter 2 on the value of compassion to sustain victory, page 55); tell them you know how it must feel to lose or fail and how important they are to the team. Be kind and understanding, letting them know that you appreciate their courage to improve and risk failure. With permission to fail, they can continue to take chances to discover their greatness on the roller coaster of performance.

Some athletes lose confidence when they fail. That's why it's crucial to define success multidimensionally rather than just by outcomes and results. When they lose a game or match or race, emphasize specific ways that they did succeed in the process of the event. Athletes need to have other gauges by which they can experience victory—the little details that prove they are doing great even if the scoreboard indicates otherwise. Remember the importance of compassion in that risk-taking equation: courage to risk, plus compassion, equals success.

An athlete needs to know that what's lost by not trying and what's lost by not succeeding are two different things: encourage athletes to try, and assure them that even if they fail, ultimately they will succeed.

All skills are perfected through
the process of failure.
Embrace loss as a necessary part
of improvement.

Winning Within and Without

Jack Elway, former head coach of the Stanford Cardinal football team, was once quoted as saying that his team members were winners for years; it just didn't show on the scoreboard. USC men's basketball coach Henry Bibby claimed after a tough NCAA tournament loss that his team experienced a victory few could see. These and other very successful coaches have expanded the traditional notion of "winning" to include elements other than the outcome and results. They acknowledge that winning on the scoreboard is important, yet they emphasize equally triumphs of heart, mind, and effort. These inner triumphs are indicated by such accomplishments as overcoming odds, improving over time, exceeding personal bests (longest jump, shortest time, and so on), pushing one's body to its limit, and reaching one's potential. Such victories over self-doubt, fear, failure, and ego are often the precursor and prerequisite of triumph on the field.

Coaches play a huge part in helping athletes (and teams as a whole) discover this deeper, perhaps more fulfilling aspect of winning by showing them that there are many ways to achieve, to win. This section magnifies for you some specific ways you can do this and can focus on alternate, personal winnings. Naturally, the concepts presented in preceding pages regarding how to learn and therefore "win" by losing are a crucial part of this message.

Consider successful coach Geno Auriemma, who keeps his University of Connecticut women's basketball teams at the highest levels. He obviously loves to win. Still, winning is not everything for Coach Auriemma; doing the right thing is. He takes special care to recruit players who share his philosophies and commitments. He teaches athletes that winning is not just the final score, but is also about pushing yourself to execute, to do things the way they're supposed to be done. If you do that, high-level results are the natural by-product. According to Auriemma, you need to repeat this process over and over and it will happen. This is true inner winning—getting it done right.

Such inner victory was experienced by head coach Alan Kirkup with his Arkansas women's soccer team against the second-ranked University of Florida Gators in the conference playoffs. Thought to have no chance even to be on the same field as the Gators, his tough, gutsy Razorbacks played terrific ball in a tight 4-3 loss. This inner victory gave them more confidence and sparked their enthusiasm for the next season; it gave them an opportunity to play a tough opponent and prove to themselves that they could play with the best. When they let go of the expectation of having to win, they relaxed and played a superb game; they played with their hearts and put it all on the line, getting a glimpse of how great they could be.

Focus on Small Steps

Who doesn't love to win? This is, after all, why we keep score. Winning allows us to measure success more objectively. But an overemphasis on winning can exert undue pressure on coaches and players, and can clutter the room they need to grow emotionally, mentally, spiritually, or physically in order to find new ways to improve their performance.

Often the integrity of an athletic program is lost when winning becomes its sole obsession. A 1990 *Sports Illustrated* interview with Allegheny College president Daniel Sullivan addressed this issue. He gave the following statement: "I cannot think of a single thing that has eroded public confidence in America's colleges and universities . . . more than intercollegiate athletics as practiced by a large faction of the universities in the NCAA's Divisions I and II. It is hard to teach integrity in the pursuit of knowledge or how to live a life of purpose and service when an institution's own integrity is compromised in the unconstrained pursuit of victory on the playing fields (page 38)." By contrast, the athletic department at Allegheny, he said, enjoys winning, yet understands the role of sport in creating joy and fun while developing the athlete's potential as a human being. This philosophy is an integral part of the department's mission statement.

When we need to win to feel validated in what we do, we build up layers of anxiety and stress because we have no control over the outcomes. At that point, the prospect of winning becomes short-lived. To change this, focus athletes on winning in those things they can control—their skills, plays, attitudes, and mind-sets. Emphasize the multidimensional nature of victory. Where traditional victory is transitory, outstanding performances last a lifetime.

Successful, creative coaches I work with keep track of athletes who make small steps toward performing better in practice and games. At the end of a practice session the staff takes time to talk about those athletes who did exceptional work and to reward them for their hard work, diligent effort, and commitment to high standards—all ways to win. You can help your athletes to tune in to this philosophy by talking about it from day one and having your staff keep track of these items during practice sessions as well as games. Athletes need to know that you are watching how they perform in this way. You may want to consider an athlete of the week award, given to that athlete who demonstrates deeper levels of winning, exhibiting all-around good effort, spirit, and sportsmanship.

> *Define winning as an athlete's willingness*
> *to commit to performing certain tasks*
> *that are indicative of high levels of play.*

Ask Athletes the Right Questions

Don't confuse letting go of the need to win with not wanting to win. "Needing to win" means that's all there is to it; this takes away from the true rewards resulting from excellent performance and the fine execution of well-thought-out plans. To help athletes let go of this need, coaches can encourage them to ask the right questions before play.

Traditionally, athletes wonder, "What do we need to do?" The answer is often related to outcomes—for example, "We need to score to win," or "beat the opponent," or "go for the title." Because we can't control these outcomes, we flirt with self-doubt, fear, and stress, and performance suffers as a result. Encourage athletes to ask instead, "How do we need to be?" The answer helps them to concentrate on behaviors they can control in the present; they can choose to be bold, fearless, tenacious, relaxed, fluid, prepared, enthusiastic, and courageous. As you may recall from chapter 7, focusing on these strengths keeps athletes relaxed, confident, and empowered. When we free ourselves to be all that we are capable of, we raise the bar on our own performance.

You also can help your athletes to win when you ask, "What does it mean to play with intensity? Can you go out and demonstrate what this 'going all out' looks like?" Have them visualize intensity by feeling "the feeling of going all out" and then replicating it for five minutes. Use this experience as a reference point when you want them to access this feeling in the future. In a meeting called for this purpose, ask athletes what it means to be courageous, bold, and daring . . . to be enthusiastic and excited. Ask them, "How do you demonstrate that?"

Play Like Champions

In a similar forum, you can ask athletes if they are willing to play like champions. Have them define what championship-level play is by identifying four traits, behaviors, or actions of a champion. For example, a champion will dive for the loose ball, sprint up on offense, sprint back on defense, and never give up regardless of the score. Every sport is different, yet athletes all win when they play like winners. All the teams and athletes I've worked with have used these questions and adapted the answers to their progress with enormous success.

Once you define those particular traits of champions, ask each athlete to identify those that they would like to adapt for themselves. Then ask them to prove how serious they are about playing like a winner by committing to executing these traits every time they set foot on the playing field. Draw up a contract and have them sign it (see chapter 7, page 141). At a specific team meeting, collect all responses and have all players read one another's tasks as a way to establish accountability. This is best accomplished after they have a few games or competitions under their belts and have a better idea of their current level of performance. This exercise could hold for a season or could be repeated again when the athletes have mastered these traits.

Finally, have everyone affirm, "We may or may not win, but we play like incredible champions" (according to the team's own defined traits). This helps athletes and teams to let go of the *need* to win, and to focus instead on the essence of play. These words have been used as touchstones by numerous national champions on their roads to greatness. Olympic track athletes Regina Jacobs (1500 and 5000 meters) and Jason Pyrah (1500 meters) are two world-class runners who have adopted this affirmation on their way to winning national championships in their respective events. They each affirm, "Regardless of the outcome, I run like a strong, vibrant national champ."

At times, your athletes may be insecure about expressing their lack of confidence to you and your staff. If you think this may be the case, free them up by saying something like, "You know, it's common for all great athletes to experience a drop in confidence levels at some point in their career." This may relax them and open them up to the possibility that they also may lack confidence. Then ask them, "How can you have confidence in doing something you can't control?" Once they realize the futility in striving for the impossible, direct them toward finding confidence in what they *can* control—confidence in performing those winning traits. Encourage them not to care so much about the outcome, to just do it, and to have fun in the process. This, they will learn, is winning.

Regina Jacobs runs like a champion because she trains and thinks like a champion.

It's easy to lose confidence in winning and difficult to regain it, especially after a series of big defeats. Such was the case for speed skater Dan Jansen, who was seeded number one in the world for several years between 1984 and 1994. After three failed attempts in three consecutive Olympics at the 500-meter event, his confidence to win must have been at an all-time low. In his mind he needed to win to prove his world ranking was legitimate, but failed to do so at each Olympic final. With no more chances to win at 500 meters, his coach suggested that he race the 1,000 meters with no need to control the outcome, but to focus on being technically correct, aggressive, fluid, and to have fun. With little pressure to win, he skated like a champion, stayed focused on the process, and won the gold medal in record time in 1994. He exemplified the notion of letting go of the need to win in order to be victorious.

Confidence is easier to maintain
if athletes focus on how *they perform*
rather than whether they win.

You can help restore confidence by helping an athlete understand that he or she can exert control over a situation. Focusing on the process, as you can see, helps in this regard. Look for ways to mitigate competitive pressure for your athletes. Remind them that winning is the ability to exhibit their skills and expertise as they focus on the moment, the experience itself, rather than what the outcome may be. Such thinking, and your support for this view, will provide the best environment for an athlete to perform at her best. You may also decide to experiment like Dan Jansen did and have your athletes take on events, positions, or roles that are not normally theirs. Tell them to just do it and to enjoy the opportunity to perform with no expectation regarding outcome.

- When I help my athletes see loss as gain, they experience higher levels of performance. I teach them to embrace their setbacks on the road to success.

- When I help my athletes to focus on the process of playing rather than the need to win, they improve their chances for victory.

John Wooden said it perfectly in *Wooden:* "The dividend [winning] is not necessarily in outscoring an opponent. The guaranteed dividend is the complete peace of mind gained in knowing you did everything within your power, physically, mentally, and emotionally, to bring forth your potential" (page 130).

10

Implementing Mental Tactics

Don't work harder, work smarter. Let your opponents overwork themselves as you prepare wisely to strike when rested.

Well-respected coaches successfully employ invaluable mental tactics in a wide variety of sports, including basketball, football, soccer, lacrosse, hockey, volleyball, tennis, track, swimming, vaulting, rowing, skydiving, and cycling. These strategies put the finishing touches on the process of unleashing athletes who are prepared to take risks, cope with failure, learn from loss, win in the process, and demonstrate their potential. In short, this chapter discusses simple tactical mental maneuvers that help athletes and teams gain a competitive advantage before the contest begins. Reserve these strategies for those athletes who have repeatedly demonstrated an ability to focus on their own game and what they can control. Once they have honed their ability to block out distractions, they can sharpen their edge against opponents using the simple methods of deceiving or surprising opponents, learning to adapt to many circumstances, and stabilizing their emotions.

Deceiving Your Opponents

Legendary coach Hank Iba once said that "the essence of the game is deception." The art of deception is one of many strategic tactics described thousands of years ago in one of the most widely read books on strategy, Sun-Tzu's *The Art of War.* The rule of thumb in deceiving your opponents effectively is to show them something contrary to your plan, or contrary to what truly is. The key to gaining this advantage is to know your opponent while remaining unknown to them. The deception comes in fooling your opponents, but not your own athletes. It is crucial to ensure that your athletes are not confusing this rhetoric of deception with their own positive affirmations. The athlete wants his opponent to think he is weak or not ready to play, yet the athlete knows otherwise. Emphasize to the team that these thoughts are for the media and rivals to absorb, that they are separate from the teams' positive affirmations. Be sure that, aside from the deception, your players spend less energy and attention on the opponent and focus more on what they can control, what they can do, and how they need to be in the heat of competition. Deceptive moves are usually subtle and simple, yet powerful.

*Appear to your opponent as ineffective and
less competent; be unknown to them.
Show what is contrary so that no one
can tell what you are doing.*

I work with a national-class cyclist who makes excellent use of this psychological tactic. Before a race begins, he uses body language that communicates to his opponent that he is really no threat. By doing so he relaxes his competitors, placing him in position to act unexpectedly. He then creates a false sense of weakness. He'll say, "I'm tired; I've had no rest," or "I haven't been on the bike in a week," or "My back is sore." Hearing this, his competitors expect him to have an off day. He talks about his own sense of vulnerability while at the same time praising his competitors and building them up. He gives the appearance of being unfit and not prepared, which contributes to his opponents' feeling hopeful and overconfident. They take him lightly and relax.

He then strikes with lightning speed, dropping everyone behind in the process.

Some coaches I've known use this tactic creatively with their teams by playing up injuries to key players or showing certain offenses to some teams only to display something entirely new for a big game. These same coaches do not hesitate to build up the opponent, telling the media how strong they are and that they are "the team to beat," hoping the opposing team will become so smitten with themselves that they will take the game lightly.

Surprising Your Opponents

Another powerful tactic is the surprise factor, which keeps your opponent guessing where the strike will take place. Unlike deception, when you present information to your opponent or the media that could be misleading, with the element of surprise you simply conceal what you have by not leaking any important information to your opponent. It requires a posture of mystery, one in which your offense strikes where your opponent least expects it. Throwing in a new game plan, one that couldn't be detected through scouting reports, is effective. Dean Smith orchestrated the four-corners stall years ago, surprised everyone, and changed the world of basketball.

If you can keep your opponents unaware of your plan, you can increase the chances of victory. Sun-Tzu calls it *genius,* the ability to surprise opponents with change and variable formations, causing them to constantly adapt. You should, however, be wary of letting the surprise element become so complicated that your athletes lose sight of just playing the game and performing their best. For example, as a track or cross-country coach, you could unleash a new race strategy, having athletes surge where normally others would not. Many Kenyan runners, including Henry Rono, have used this strategy effectively. Henry would run with the pack and then, unexpectedly, would throw in a tremendous surge, leaving others in the dust. He would then back off, creating the illusion to his competitors that they were catching back up to him. As they narrowed the gap and started to feel good about their chances, he would bolt once again and completely discourage his competitors.

North Carolina's coach Dean Smith demonstrated the effectiveness of doing the unexpected.

Learning to Adapt

Adaptation is another effective tactic that suggests not holding to a fixed plan of attack but changing according to the unfolding of events. When you are too rigid, you can break. Being flexible and adapting to change, on the other hand, keeps you fluid and allows you to adjust and rise above the change. Those who adapt maintain the advantage. All athletes should be able to learn how to adapt. As a coach, you can create situations in practice where you enable the offense to adapt to shifts in the defense. Adaptation is a learned behavior, grasped by athletes when they have the opportunity to react to changing situations in practice first and then discuss with the coach how a reaction was or was not effective in the given situation. From this discussion, athletes and coaches can determine the most effective way to adapt in a similar competitive situation. Thinking through such situations not only helps athletes and coaches plan ahead, but also gets them accustomed to adapting to game situations that may subvert an athlete's original "plan."

Adaptation requires you to shift your plans and mind-sets when the change happens. For example, a game is changed from a dirt field to turf. Sunny, warm weather turns to cold rain. Sport is predictably unpredictable, and those who adapt well perform well. Athletes need to practice the ability to be flexible and "go with the flow." Such ability and the knowledge that change won't be a hindrance result in a clear psychological advantage in competition. Any form of resistance to change causes tension, anxiety, and stress, which will detract from performance.

When others use surprise on you,
be prepared to adapt to any change.
Be flexible and go with the flow.

You, too, can help athletes adapt by anticipating and preparing for certain shifts in competitive situations. Knowing that her team might have to play on a dry field (they were used to playing on a wet turf, which helps stop the ball from bouncing), one coach had her field hockey team practice under various field conditions before their championship tournament. Having this experience not only helped the team to adapt, it increased their confidence to know they could play well either way. The team did have to play a championship match on a dry surface and won, thanks to the foresight of the coach.

Sometimes a team or athlete needs to adapt without prior planning. For example, sometimes championship finals can change at the last minute due to TV programming shifts. That has happened in the case of many Olympic finals. Imagine being on the track, preparing to run your event, when you are told that the event will be run an hour later than anticipated. All runners in the race have to go into a holding pattern. With nerves frayed and anticipation running high, many athletes might lose their focus and spend energy becoming upset. The athlete who takes the delay in stride and adapts by finding a way to use that time positively (meditating, relaxing, and visualizing the race) will have a distinct advantage over his opponents. A coach can effectively prepare an athlete by anticipating possible surprises—weather factors, delays due to TV scheduling, changes in lane assignment, and so on—and having the athlete mentally rehearse positive responses weeks in advance of the event. This enables the athlete to be calm when faced with change.

If you teach adaptation and flexibility in your pregame message to your athletes, the athletes will be more relaxed when change occurs. A simple reminder during a competitive situation can help athletes to respond quickly to any change. In a closely contested basketball playoff game, a power failure halted the game for 45 minutes. The score was tied at the time of the delay. One astute coach gathered his team, took them to the locker room, and had them visualize themselves still playing at their best while the other team simply stood around waiting for the power to come back. When the lights came on and the game resumed, the team who had visualized reeled off 10 unanswered points and ran away with the game. Their opponents had lost their focus.

Start training your athletes to accept changing situations and to adapt successfully to them by identifying the possible factors or setbacks that could happen during competition. Remind your athletes that when the unexpected happens, it's important for them to remain focused, but also to stay flexible and go with the flow. Reflect on your experience and on situations that you and your team have had to adapt to before. Have them experience as many of these situations as they can in a practice situation, where possible—for example, practicing in a variety of weather and playing surface conditions.

It is impossible to simulate all eventualities. The best way to plan for something unpredictable is to not be afraid to adapt. If you talk to your team about the importance of adjusting to any change, when it does happen they will be better prepared to shift, regardless of the particular change, and will feel confident about doing so. Then, when an opponent throws up a surprise offense or defense, you can simply remind them that this is a time to be flexible and go with the flow. Have them visualize adapting to the circumstances. Rigid, tight athletes eventually crack; flexible, adaptable athletes bend, blend, and find their way to the top.

Stabilizing Your Emotions

As a rule, athletes create a huge advantage over an opponent when they appear unemotional, calm, and detached, even though fire may rage within. I call this *relaxed intensity,* and it applies to both coaches and athletes. Becoming outwardly angry, frustrated, or upset (although at times this may not be preventable) is a sure indication of your loss of control and an admission that the opponent is getting in your head. Athletes, particularly in individual sports, begin to walk the path of defeat when they emotionally fall apart. Such expressions of these emotions create instability and distraction. Strategically, it's wise to function outside the sphere of emotional captivity. You see this in golf and tennis all the time. An athlete breaks a club or throws a racket and the opponent smiles (even if only on the inside), knowing she will triumph.

This also includes getting too involved with the "rah, rah" posture, which often is just a show of a team's need to convince themselves and their opponents that they are ready. Excessive emotionalism, as with most excess, can result in fatigue, distraction, indecisiveness, confusion, nervousness, and inner instability. Let any outward expression of emotion be the result of the passion and intensity overflowing onto the field of play. After a very intense performance and win in cross-country mountain biking, national champion and Olympian Travis Brown threw up his arms and grinned like a big kid as he crossed the finish line. His emotional display was his release after a tough, challenging race.

- We use surprise—through change and inconsistent attacks—to conceal our advantages over our opponents.
- I remain unemotional, calm, and detached on the surface when possible.

Using these psychological tactics, as well as constantly reinforcing the concepts of winning, losing, and competing, will help you, as a creative coach, to unleash athletes who are ready to enter the arena of competition and to perform at their best on every outing.

references
and resources

Associated Press (New York). 1996. Interview with Pete Sampras as reported on June 27. Cited on www.canoe.ca.

Bradley, Bill. 1998. *Values of the Game*. New York: Artisan.

Cleary, Thomas, trans. 1996. *The Book of Leadership and Strategy*, ed. Emily Bower. Boston: Shambala.

Dreher, Diane, and Lao-Tzu Tao Te Chung. 1997. *The Tao of Personal Leadership*. New York: Harper Collins.

Hannula, Dick, and Nort Thornton, eds. In press. *The Swim Coaching Bible*. Champaign, IL: Human Kinetics.

Jackson, Phil, and Hugh Delahanty. 1996. *Sacred Hoops: Spiritual Lessons of a Hardwood Warrior*. New York: Hyperion.

Leonard, George Burr. 1975. *The Ultimate Athlete*. 1st ed. New York: Viking.

Libby, Bill. 1972. *The Coaches*. Chicago: Henry Regnery Company.

Looney, Douglas S. 1990. More than a win. *Sports Illustrated* **73**(25), Dec. 17, 38-39.

Lynch, Jerry, and C.L. Huang. 1999. *Tao Mentoring*. New York: Marlowe and Co.

Sun-Tzu. 1984. *The Art of War*. New York: Delacorte.

Suzuki, Shunryu. 1988. *Zen Mind, Beginner's Mind*. Trumbull, CT: Weatherhill.

Wooden, John R. 1997. *Wooden*. Chicago: NTC/Contemporary.

index

Note: Photographs are indicated by italicized page numbers.

about the author

Jerry Lynch, PhD, is founder and director of the TaoSports Center for Athletic Development in Santa Cruz, California. A sport psychologist for more than 20 years, he has worked with numerous Olympic, national, collegiate, and professional coaches and athletes. He was a U.S. regional and national champion distance runner and has coached at the high school level and youth sport level.

Lynch has published seven books, including *Running Within* (Human Kinetics, 1999), and the perennial bestsellers *Working Out, Working Within* and *Thinking Body, Dancing Mind: TaoSports for Extraordinary Performance in Athletics, Business and Life*, which is available in seven languages. These books have been used by athletes and coaches of the San Antonio Spurs, Chicago Bulls, Detroit Pistons, and Cleveland Cavaliers. Lynch has clients in the PGA, NFL, and NBA; he has worked with numerous NCAA championship teams as well as with athletic programs worldwide. He regularly conducts coaching clinics throughout the United States.

Lynch has written feature articles in numerous journals and national magazines. His work has been written about in *Sports Illustrated* and featured in the *New York Times, Washington Post,* and other periodicals. He is also a contributor to the Medical & Training Advice column in *Runner's World*, a columnist for *VeloNews,* and a contributing editor and writer with Asimba.com. Lynch resides in Santa Cruz, California, with his wife, Jan, and their four children. He can be reached via e-mail at **Taosports@aol.com**.